OUR LOST CONSTITUTION

SENATOR
MIKE LEE

OUR LOST CONSTITUTION

The Willful Subversion of America's Founding Document

SENTINEL

SENTINEL

Published by the Penguin Group
Penguin Group (USA) LLC
375 Hudson Street
New York, New York 10014

USA | Canada | UK | Ireland | Australia | New Zealand | India | South Africa | China
penguin.com
A Penguin Random House Company

First published by Sentinel, a member of Penguin Group (USA) LLC, 2015

ISBN 978-1-59184-777-9

Printed in the United States of America
1 3 5 7 9 10 8 6 4 2

Set in Adobe Caslon

To Sharon

CONTENTS

Author's Note   *ix*

Introduction   *1*

CHAPTER 1

Ducking and Dodging the Constitution   7

PART I
THE LOST CLAUSES

CHAPTER 2

The Compromise That Saved the Constitutional Convention . . .
and That Should Have Saved Us from Obamacare

The Forgotten Origination Clause   *17*

CHAPTER 3

From Congress to a King

The Forgotten Legislative Powers Clause   *47*

CHAPTER 4

The Supreme Court's Klansman

The Forgotten Establishment Clause   *77*

CHAPTER 5

Liberty: "A Reality or a Shadow"?

The Forgotten Fourth Amendment   *103*

CHAPTER 6
"But Structure Means Liberty"
The Forgotten Tenth Amendment and the Inflated
Commerce Clause   *131*

PART II
RECLAIMING THE LOST CLAUSES

CHAPTER 7
Reclaiming the Constitution Through the Courts   *157*

CHAPTER 8
Reclaiming the Constitution Through Legislation   *175*

CHAPTER 9
Reclaiming the Constitution Through the Power
of the Purse   *187*

CHAPTER 10
What *You* Can Do to Reclaim the Constitution   *199*

Acknowledgments   *217*
Notes   *219*
Index   *235*

AUTHOR'S NOTE

IN *THE KILLER ANGELS*, MICHAEL SHAARA REMINDS READERS
that Stephen Crane wrote *The Red Badge of Courage* "because reading the cold history was not enough; he wanted to know what it was
like to be there, what the weather was like, what men's faces looked
like." He warns his readers, "You may find it a different story from
the one you learned in school."[1]

I hope this book tells a different story from the one you learned
in school, even if (perhaps especially if) your school was a law
school. I don't purport to be another Shaara or Crane. But like
them, I wanted to give readers some glimpse into "what it was like
to be there." What was it like to live under King George's tyranny?
What was it like for those who participated in the "miracle in Philadelphia" and produced our Constitution? If this book succeeds, it
will help you feel as if you were right there at the pivotal moments
of history, experiencing the rise and the fall of the constitutional
provisions that I call the "Lost Constitution."

To that end, I have taken some dramatic license on several occasions in telling these historical backstories. In no instance have I
knowingly departed from what I have found in the historical record.
But I have, for example, imagined what Alexander Hamilton might
have said when he confronted a lynch mob at his college. And I have
imagined some of what might have transpired behind closed doors
at a dinner and special session of the Philadelphia Convention when

Ben Franklin proposed the compromise that saved the Constitution.

At the outset of this project, I expected to use far more dramatic license than I have taken. In the course of my research, I was pleasantly surprised to find that the historical record is more dramatic than anything I could have imagined. It is also far more illuminating. As a result, with only a few exceptions, I found myself writing not historical fiction but history.

OUR LOST CONSTITUTION

INTRODUCTION

MY LOVE FOR THE U.S. CONSTITUTION TOOK ROOT IN MY EARLY years. From the time I was a young child, my parents taught me about the separation of powers, checks and balances, due process, equal protection, and the limited role of our federal government. It never really occurred to me that I was being taught about the Constitution; these were just conversations we had from time to time around the dinner table, in the car, and whenever the subject of government happened to arise. Before long, I learned what it meant to be an appellate lawyer because every time my siblings or I would disagree with our parents' decisions about bedtimes or chores or allowances, they would say, "Make your case. You're probably not going to win, but we'll listen."[1]

When I was about ten years old, I started routinely accompanying my dad whenever he argued cases before the U.S. Supreme Court. As kind and wise a man as I've ever known, he was the founding dean of BYU's law school, and in 1981 he became the solicitor general of the United States, the federal government's chief advocate before the Supreme Court. I'd watch with bated breath as the black-robed justices fired questions at him. He had a way of answering their questions in a manner that was not only responsive but also carefully calculated to advance his case. The verbal jousting I saw between lawyers and justices wasn't quite as raucous as the debates at our dinner table, but after the oral argument ended, my dad would be so excited that he reminded me of a giddy child on a sugar high.[2]

My dad didn't win every argument at the Supreme Court, but he did win most of them. More important, however, he had a near-perfect batting average at home. He could simplify even the most complicated of concepts, and I hung on his every word. I didn't always understand everything he said, but I sure made an effort—especially because he had a way of making almost any subject seem interesting, and he loved it when any of his children showed genuine interest in the Constitution. I still remember how pleased he seemed when, as a fourth grader, I replied to his explanation of America's long-standing abortion debate by asking, "Shouldn't this issue be addressed by the states rather than by the federal courts?"

My dad could hardly contain his joy. I was only nine or ten years old.

A year or two later, the same issue arrived at our front door—literally. It was a cold morning in March. My parents had taken my three younger sisters shopping. My older brother was at a basketball game. The only people in the house were me and my older sister Wendy; and because she was still asleep, I was the only one who saw the most peculiar of vehicles pulling up in front of our house: a huge Greyhound bus.

Ours was a quiet suburban street in McLean, Virginia, many miles from the nearest bus stop. But even more unusual than the bus was the behavior of the dozens of people who poured out of it. I watched with wide-eyed curiosity as they began pacing the sidewalk in front of our house. They seemed to be chanting something, but exactly what I wasn't sure. Determined to figure out what was happening, I went outside, which made it easier for me to see and hear what they were saying. Their chant was simple and consistent with the words written on the signs they were carrying: "Keep your laws off our bodies!"

Immediately, mischievous thoughts flowed through my eleven-year-old mind. *Should I turn on the sprinklers?* I wondered. *Should I deploy my secret stash of firecrackers?* Like the boy in *Home Alone*, I instinctively felt the need to defend my parents' home, and startling these protesters sounded like an awfully fun way to do it.

Fortunately, I was (barely) mature enough to resist my first instincts. *If I do that, it'll be on the news,* I thought. *That will end up caus-ing problems for my dad, and I don't want to do that.*

Instead, I decided to calmly approach and speak to the strangers who had arrived without invitation or warning on our sidewalk. I found the woman who appeared to be in charge and said, "I live in this house. Can you tell me why you're here?"

"Well, little boy," she said in the most condescending way imag-inable, "we're not here to hurt you. We just really disagree with some of the things that your daddy is doing in his job."

It can be a little jarring when the first thing people tell you is that they don't mean you any harm. That's sometimes the first indication that the opposite is true.

In this case, I knew enough about my dad's job and the abortion debate to realize they were angry about arguments he had presented to the Supreme Court. I later learned that the case was *City of Akron v. Akron Center for Reproductive Health*, a case involving the consti-tutionality of a city ordinance requiring second- and third trimester abortions to be performed in hospitals and requiring minors to ob-tain either parental or judicial consent before obtaining an abortion. Appearing on behalf of the U.S. government (as *amicus curiae* or "friend of the court"), my father argued that, in adjudicating such constitutional questions, the Supreme Court should give due defer-ence to states and local legislative bodies, especially where fact-laden questions of public policy are concerned. But that still didn't explain why these people were in front of my house.

"That's fine," I said, "but why do you have to do it here? Why do you have to do it in my front yard?" After all, their signs said, "Keep your laws off our bodies." Was it too much to ask them to keep their bodies off our lawn?

Apparently it was. She told me, "We're being very careful not to step on your grass. I'm sure that you have lots of fun playing with your friends out here. We're just staying on the sidewalk."

Boy, I thought to myself, *she is really missing my point.* I wasn't concerned about the grass. My concern went beyond the technical distinction between private property and public easements. I had meant to make a fairly obvious point: You can disagree with people, but that doesn't mean you should go where they sleep and eat and raise children, attempting to subject them and their families to public shame, scorn, and humiliation.

After a while, a concerned neighbor found me and asked, "Hey, are you okay? Are you scared?"

But as soon as he saw the smile on my face, he knew I was just fine. I loved discussing important questions of public policy, and my usual sparring partners at the dinner table were a lot tougher to debate than the obtuse protester on my sidewalk. While I was a little startled, I was having the time of my life.

For the next two hours, men, women, and even a few children— apparently oblivious to the irony, they had brought *children* to an abortion-rights protest—marched up and down our sidewalk, always careful not to step on the grass. A news crew came and went. Neighbors gawked inquisitively from time to time, but the whole affair didn't seem to hold anyone's attention very long—including that of the protesters themselves. The sign-wielding activists whose voices became so familiar to me that day eventually grew tired of waiting for their much-anticipated, face-to-face confrontation with my father, who was still running errands with my mom and my three younger sisters. With disappointment showing on their faces, they climbed back into their bus and called it a day.

Within seconds after they left, my parents pulled into the driveway. In a stroke of bad luck for the protesters—who had traveled all the way from New York and New Jersey to criticize my father—they had missed him by less than two minutes.

I was standing next to the basketball goal at the end of our driveway, chomping at the bit to tell my parents about all the excitement they'd missed. But before I could get out a word, my dad beat me to the punch. "There was a huge Greyhound bus going out of the neighborhood," he said with a baffled look on his face. "Do you know anything about that?"

Although I disagree with the message of those protesters and believe they should have found a more appropriate place to march than the private residence of a public official, I admire their passion. At least they cared about the Constitution and the essential role it plays in limiting the power of government. At least they were willing to view government action with a critical eye, refusing to ignore what they perceived as a constitutional overreach. I wish more Americans—even those who read the Constitution differently than I do—shared their passion for identifying and enforcing constitutional limits on the power of government.

I wrote this book for people who share my lifelong love of the Constitution and my growing frustration with legislators, judges, and presidents who ignore and distort it. In one sense, this is a book about heroes and villains—those who inspired, crafted, and respected liberty's safeguards and those who have tried to tear those safeguards down. But in another sense, this is a book with a message: The "Lost Constitution" should be restored, and it can be, but only if we remember the people and the stories behind it.

My wish for you is that you share your time not with me but with them.

CHAPTER 1

Ducking and Dodging
the Constitution

I KEEP TWO TOWERS OF DOCUMENTS IN MY SENATE OFFICE. THE
first is only a few inches tall. A collection of all the legislation passed
by Congress in 2013, it contains about eight hundred pages.

The second tower, which is *eleven feet tall*, is a collection of regulations proposed and adopted by federal agencies in 2013. It contains
about *eighty thousand* pages.

These extraordinarily unequal towers illustrate a startling reality:
The U.S. Congress no longer passes most of the federal laws, rules,
and regulations that are imposed on the American people. While a
mountain of those rules are decreed by an army of unelected federal
bureaucrats, only about 1 percent of the rules we must live by are enacted by the most accountable branch of government—Congress.

Using a classic duck-and-dodge strategy, Congress routinely en-
acts legislation that purports to solve a genuine problem but provides
no specific solutions. Congress then delegates to executive-branch
bureaucrats the power to make legally binding rules or "regulations,"
which will themselves determine the law's real-world impact. It's a
brilliant plan; Congress gets all the credit for the popular goal and
none of the blame for the controversial particulars of regulation.

One prominent example of this kind of lawmaking can be found in the Clean Air Act. The act essentially declares that "we shall have clean air" and then outlines a broad vision for limiting air pollution from both mobile sources (like cars) and stationary sources (like factories). The act contains relatively few details as to how its laudable objectives will be achieved. Instead, it authorizes the Environmental Protection Agency (EPA) to make and enforce legally binding regulations that, far more than the act itself, restrict air pollution.

This approach certainly has its advantages, and few would dispute that America's air quality has improved substantially since the Clean Air Act's passage and implementation. I'm happy, as I assume all Americans are, that the Clean Air Act has improved our nation's air quality. There is, however, a major problem with this method of lawmaking: It insulates lawmakers from voter accountability and thereby undermines one of our Constitution's most important features. It insulates members of Congress by giving them plausible deniability; they can blame the executive agencies for anything the voters don't like. The bureaucrats at those agencies, in turn, become a unique and privileged class of lawmakers; they are insulated from voter accountability because they are *never* required to stand for election.

Thus, when the EPA adopts a new regulation carrying the force of law, those who find that law unnecessary, unreasonable, or even harmful are left with little recourse. Understandably, they might complain to those who have been elected to represent them in Congress. Members of Congress instinctively respond to such complaints by expressing empathy for those harmed by the law and frustration with the EPA and then adding something like "Well, that regulation was put in place by the EPA. That is where you should take your complaint." Of course, the people at the EPA—as hardworking, well educated, and well intentioned as they may be—

tend not to be terribly concerned about citizen complaints because they cannot be voted out of office.

It can be hard for most Americans—that is, those who don't work in Congress or monitor its operations on a full-time basis—to understand how far our government has drifted from the Constitution's vision and in many cases its actual stated provisions. Many Americans probably assume that our lawmakers understand our founding document and are devoted to defending it. Unfortunately, that assumption is in many ways incorrect.

Far too many members of Congress don't understand the Constitution they've sworn to defend—not because they *can't* understand it but because they make little or no effort to do so. Some Supreme Court justices aren't much better; too many of them understand our founding document but refuse to acknowledge that its most important function is to limit and check power. Presidents are often even worse; they pay lip service to our nation's governing document with their words, but their actions frequently betray a lack of real commitment to its restrictions.

People serving in each of these positions have raised their right hands and sworn some variation of an oath "to preserve, protect, and defend the Constitution of the United States." Most, if not all, of the people who have made such a vow intended at the outset to keep it. Maybe they believe they are keeping it. But far too often they are not. The truth is that our Constitution is being subverted by many of the very people who have solemnly promised to protect it.

Most of the destruction is done by well-meaning government officials who believe that our governing document is more of a starting point than a necessary set of boundaries. Those who espouse this view tend to profess a kind of reverence for the Constitution but talk about its restrictive structure with a combination of detachment and disdain. They make it clear that they think the idea of restraining government power by means of a written governing document is a topic better suited for an ancient-history class than for a contemporary political discussion. Adherents to this viewpoint will occasionally say that the Constitution was crafted by and for an "agrarian society"—meaning that it is a sort of quaint document written for a society that is nothing like our own. As far as these critics are concerned, we don't need to follow a bunch of rigid rules put in place by Americans who grew their own food and whose most sophisticated mode of transportation involved a horse and buggy.

When I arrived in Washington, I found it awash with people who viewed the Constitution as a nuisance. There was an attorney general who, contradicting experts within his own Department of Justice, vouched for the constitutionality of a legislative proposal that would give the District of Columbia representation in Congress, even though the Constitution makes clear that only *states* are entitled to such representation. There was a president who had bullied and badgered the Supreme Court after it issued a free-speech decision with which he disagreed. And there was an outgoing Speaker of the House who, when asked which provision of the Constitution gives Congress authority to make Americans buy health insurance, answered with scorn and incredulity by simply replying, "Are you serious? Are you *serious?*"[1]

Rather than considering the Constitution important enough for their consideration, many senators and congressmen now punt constitutional questions to staff, who in turn defer (often excessively) to the courts in construing the Constitution. If you ask senators or congressmen about the constitutionality of a particular legislative proposal, they might well answer, "Experts on my staff have assured me that, if this bill becomes law, the courts will not invalidate it."

Relying on court decisions is no substitute for legitimate, independent constitutional analysis, which should take place within every branch of government. Every elected official has an affirmative, independent obligation to act within the Constitution's limits, regardless of whether courts are likely to intervene. Lawmakers who don't move beyond the question of what the courts will permit are like children trying to get away with a kind of rule breaking their parents aren't likely to catch.

It was this state of affairs that convinced me to run for the U.S. Senate in 2010, challenging a three-term incumbent from my own party. It bothered me that even in the Republican Party, far too many elected officials have been reluctant to engage the public in a meaningful constitutional discourse. Although the GOP purports to stand for principles of constitutionally limited government, not every Republican lawmaker is willing to engage in a thoughtful constitutional dialogue—one that attempts to identify limits on federal power and extends beyond a facile assessment of how likely the courts might be to invalidate a particular law.

Sometimes government officials overlook serious constitutional defects in a legislative proposal because they see that some features of the proposal may be popular. It is politically advantageous for them to defer all constitutional questions to the courts, which can then carry all responsibility (and any accompanying blame) for the proposal's unconstitutionality. President George W. Bush, for example, signed the Bipartisan Campaign Reform Act of 2002 (also known as the McCain-Feingold Act), even though he knew major parts of it violated Americans' right to free speech. He explained that "certain provisions present serious constitutional concerns"; that "questions arise under the First Amendment" regarding a limit on individual campaign contributions; and that he had "reservations about the constitutionality" of another major provision restricting political advertising.[2] But in a shocking abrogation of his constitutional duty to defend the Constitution, Bush signed the bill, meekly explaining, "I expect that the courts will resolve these legitimate legal questions as appropriate under the law."[3] In so doing, he forced upon the American people an onerous set of legal obligations that he himself recognized were constitutionally infirm. Americans had to either humbly submit to an unconstitutional law or go through the time-consuming, expensive, and politically risky exercise of challenging the law in court.

Eight years after Bush acknowledged this law's constitutional defects but refused to veto it, the Supreme Court invalidated parts of it. Liberals went wild, demanding a constitutional amendment to repeal part of the First Amendment and heaping on the Court the criticism that Bush had deflected and that continues to this day.

Even though the Supreme Court righted some of Bush's wrongs, many of our constitutional rights cannot (or, for one reason or another, will not) be addressed by the courts. To put it simply, the Constitution has to be defended by all three branches of government. Now more than ever, we need our elected officials to think about these things and enforce provisions of the Constitution that courts have not been willing to enforce.

Our Lost Constitution tells the stories behind some of the most important of those provisions. Each of the chapters in part 1 describes the story behind the rise and fall of a particular constitutional provision. Why was that provision included in the Constitution? What does it mean? And how did we forget it? In every case, the clause at issue fell victim to the dangerous and deliberate choices of powerful people—some well intentioned, others more malevolent—who put their own agendas above the fundamental values of our Constitution.

Part 2 explains how the Constitution's lost clauses can be brought back to life. Each of part 2's chapters describes a different mechanism for resurrecting the Lost Constitution—from the power litigants have demonstrated in their fight for the Second Amendment to the potential for legislators to rein in executive abuse by controlling the purse and passing new laws to the importance of voters making informed choices based on candidates' commitment to aggressively protect the Constitution they will (if elected) swear to uphold. No single one of these mechanisms is sufficient. We will reclaim our Constitution only when litigants, judges, elected officials, and (most important) voters decide that the Lost Constitution must not remain lost forever.

PART I

The Lost Clauses

CHAPTER 2

The Compromise That Saved the Constitutional Convention . . . and That Should Have Saved Us from Obamacare

THE FORGOTTEN ORIGINATION CLAUSE

All Bills for raising Revenue shall originate in the House of Representatives; but the Senate may propose or concur with Amendments as on other Bills.

—UNITED STATES CONSTITUTION, ARTICLE I, SECTION 7

IF GAMBLERS HAD TAKEN BETS IN 1787 ABOUT THE FATE OF THE Constitutional Convention, the smart money would have been on failure. Thirteen different states—each with its own economic interests, each with its own ideological inclinations—had something to lose under a federal government able to impose taxes, pass laws, and make war, and none of them agreed on how much power to give a central government, how federal power should be divided within that government, or how much power each state should wield in choosing the officials who would run that government.

In many ways this final issue was the trickiest. The large states wanted representation in Congress to be based on the size of each state's population—the more people in a state, the more votes that state would have. The small states wanted every state to have equal representation in Congress—otherwise, they feared, the larger states would bully them. All states wanted as much power as possible, and there was only so much of it to go around.

With so many differences and divisions among the thirteen states, it is little wonder that a year after the Constitutional Convention, George Washington called the Constitution "little short of a miracle."

There is, however, something amiss about Washington's epithet. Calling the Constitution a "miracle" gives its framers too much credit—and too little. It confers *too much* credit because the process that produced the Constitution was far messier than what one would ordinarily associate with a miracle. The delegates argued with one another. They insulted one another. At times they were angry and dejected. There were days in the sweltering heat of Philadelphia when the writing of a constitution looked less like turning water into wine and more like turning swine into sausages.

In another sense, calling the Constitution a "miracle" gives its drafters *too little* credit, because miracles can seem easy. It took no time and little effort for Moses to raise his walking stick and spread his arms before the Red Sea. But making the Constitution was painfully hard. It required delegates to embrace ideological compromises and submit their states to economic sacrifices. Delegates had to accept the risks that accompany all great experiments and explorations into the unknown. And most difficult of all, every man there, no matter how educated or wealthy or esteemed, had to, in Ben Franklin's words, "doubt a little of his own infallibility" and "pay more respect to the judgment of others."[1]

At the heart of our country's creation was this impassioned acrimony, which almost sank the Constitution, and the Origination Clause, which saved it. The compromise enabled by the Origination Clause in 1787 may or may not qualify as a miracle. But Congress's willingness to evade it today is a tragedy.

Madison Waits

Alone in a Philadelphia tavern in mid-May 1787,[2] James Madison sat engrossed in a volume of Diderot's *Encyclopedia*, a gift from a friend in France—the American ambassador, Thomas Jefferson. Jefferson sent histories, biographies, and political tracts by the hundreds, and Madison consumed them as quickly as they arrived. The thirty-six-year-old Princeton graduate was still a student, and these books were his teachers.[3]

The little man with the big mind was, in the words of a colleague, "no bigger than half a piece of soap,"[4] But there was strength in the surprisingly prominent muscles that defined his face and a steeliness that was reflected not just in his all-black attire but also in his blue eyes' calm intensity. He was a quiet man but not a passive one. The wheels in his mind never stopped spinning.

In the spring of 1787, Congressman James Madison's mind focused almost exclusively on the future of his country. There were many people, both in the United States and abroad, who saw the American experiment in republican government as a failure, and painful evidence in recent years lent credence to that belief. The new nation was deeply in debt. Its economy was in shambles. Lawlessness and anarchy were on the rise. The republic's toothless federal government was distrusted and disrespected by foreign powers.

The U.S. Congress was unable to address a single one of these problems because the Articles of Confederation had created a federal government too weak to fix them. Ratified in 1777, before the bonds of union had been forged by victory over Great Britain, the Articles of Confederation constructed a loose confederation of states somewhat similar to leagues of independent nations established in Europe at the end of the Middle Ages. The Articles provided for no federal executive branch and no federal courts. Although the Articles established a Congress, it was a mere extension of state governments because state legislatures, rather than individuals, chose federal representatives. Congress could not regulate interstate commerce or raise taxes to fund the federal treasury. In fact, Congress was empowered to do little more than make *recommendations* about regulations and revenues—recommendations that each state was free to ignore.

Madison wanted to replace the Articles of Confederation with a Constitution. The new Constitution would create three branches of government, provide for representatives who would stand directly accountable to the people in their respective states, and empower Congress to raise revenues and regulate interstate commerce. To make that vision a reality, Madison had been working for the past year to persuade state legislators and his fellow congressmen to call for a constitutional convention.

After resolutions were passed by six states,[5] beginning with Madison's Virginia, Congress finally endorsed a resolution providing that "on the second Monday in May next a convention of delegates who shall have been appointed by the several states be held at Philadelphia for the sole and express purpose of revising the Articles of Confederation."[6] And that's why, in the spring of 1787, Madison was in a Philadelphia tavern—waiting.

The immediate problem for Madison was that Congress could not force the states to send delegates. The "second Monday in May" had come and gone, and thus far delegates from only two states had arrived.[7] That was nowhere near enough delegates to form a quorum of seven states for the convention Madison imagined. Nor was there any certainty that, even if enough delegates arrived, they would agree with him on the need for a strong national government. Having fought a war of independence at great cost against an intrusive central government in London, the country was suspicious of enhancing the power of a federal government hundreds of miles away from most American farms, businesses, and dinner tables.

Many thinking people, including some of his own relatives back home in Virginia, thought Madison was fighting for a lost cause. But still he waited. And waited. And waited.

He knew he didn't need every politician.

He didn't even need every state.

He only needed . . . enough.

Suddenly, the little Virginian heard the tavern door fly open and felt a welcome spring breeze waft past him. He turned his head, hoping to see a new face in the doorway, but it was just the tavern's owner. Madison returned his attention to his drink—and to his thoughts: the book from Jefferson; the nation in peril, and the men with the power to save their republic by joining his cause or to doom it by denying the people a government able to govern.

Quorum Call

As Madison studied the twenty-eight delegates in the assembly room of the Pennsylvania State House on May 25, 1787, he was elated. Around him were other brilliant minds like New York's Alexander Hamilton, patriarchs of famous families like Virginia's Edmund Randolph, and the most admired man in the Western Hemisphere, General George Washington. Although several states' delegates had not yet arrived, a quorum of seven states were represented, and the product of his patience and persistence—a "federal convention" to correct the errors of the Articles of Confederation—was finally about to begin.

The assembly room's gray walls surrounded curving rows of Windsor chairs, and green cloth covered both the small desks of the delegates and large sections of the tall windows—closed despite the summer heat to keep eavesdroppers from the secret deliberations. It was in this room, nearly eleven years earlier, that fifty-six delegates to the Second Continental Congress had defied their king and declared their new nation's independence, and quite a few of these same delegates had been here then. But as the convention was called to order, Madison's thoughts turned to the absence of some of the prior assembly's brightest stars.

Madison's friend and mentor, Thomas Jefferson, had become famous the world over for writing in that summer of independence that "all men are created equal," that they are entitled to "life, liberty, and the pursuit of happiness," and that Americans would defend those principles by pledging their "lives," their "fortunes," and their "sacred honor." But now Jefferson was thousands of miles away, serving as ambassador to France. And across the English Channel from him was the ambassador to Great Britain, John Adams. It was a pity, thought Madison, that he and his fellow delegates would have to save their country from the Articles of Confederation without two of the sharpest minds of their generation—as if the obstacles facing the convention were not already tall enough.

To create an effective government would take all the courage that had been present here in 1776, along with a virtue less necessary eleven years ago: a willingness to compromise both local self-interests for the good of the nation and firmly held beliefs for the sake of consensus. Delegates from large states would be asked to give small states more representation in Congress than their populations warranted. Delegates from small states would be asked to give up some of the disproportionate representation in Congress they currently enjoyed. And all present would need to create a stronger federal government, even though they had been educated at the altar of local control and small government.

Madison knew that concessions from each delegate would be necessary, but he was not yet sure how many principles he could in good conscience compromise. He was, in particular, wedded to the belief that because Virginia was the biggest state, it should have the most representatives in Congress. For all his many attributes, Madison did not enjoy a reputation for compromise. He was still a relatively young man, and like so many young men, he believed he had all—or at least most—of the answers.

As Madison looked around the large gray hall, the man most eager to achieve consensus in Philadelphia had not yet arrived. Forty-five years older than Madison, he was a publisher, inventor, and diplomat who had proven instrumental in the adoption of the Declaration of Independence and indispensable to America's victory over Great Britain. The eighty-one-year-old had written Pennsylvania's constitution about a decade ago and was familiar with the political wrangling required to establish a government. Although many delegates believed that his presence at the convention, in light of his age and deteriorating health, would be mostly symbolic, Madison hoped that Dr. Benjamin Franklin still had a few tricks up his sleeve.

Fortunately, Franklin's wisdom wouldn't be needed today. Warring proposals for the outlines of new constitutions would come later, as would debate over those outlines, proposed amendments to them, and then more debate over those amendments. The final stage would be the drafting of a full constitution by a "committee of style," which would put on paper the rules these men agreed should govern the government—*if* enough of them could ever agree. But all of that was the work of another day. Today's order of business was to appoint a doorkeeper, messengers, a secretary, and, most important, a chairman of the convention.

For the latter position the convention unanimously elected General George Washington.

"I Would Rather Submit to a Monarch!"

Two weeks later, on June 9, more delegates had arrived at the convention, and Madison was pleased that they shared his disaffection with the Articles of Confederation and his desire to design a more effective national government. A slim majority had reacted warmly when Edmund Randolph had introduced Madison's plan to abolish the Articles of Confederation and replace them with a new Constitution. Madison proposed to create an executive branch and a judicial branch, replace the current single house of Congress with a House of Representatives and a Senate, and empower the new national government to "legislate in all cases to which the separate States are incompetent."[8]

It wasn't until this point that a significant alternative was presented to challenge Madison's vision. But when it arose, it did so with ferocity, from the mouth of an Irish immigrant who, like Madison, was a Princeton graduate with strong opinions and a petite physique: New Jersey's William Paterson.

After a morning spent debating a proposal for state governors to elect the president—which received the support of no state's delegation—Paterson rose from his seat and delivered the convention's first rhetorical broadside. "The basis of our present authority," bellowed Paterson, "is founded on a *revision* of the articles of the present confederation." Congress and state legislatures had endorsed a "federal convention" in Philadelphia and had authorized delegates to amend the Articles of Confederation. But neither the states nor Congress had authorized the delegates to abolish the Articles and replace them with a "national" government, rather than federated government. "Can we on this ground form a national government?" asked Paterson. "I fancy not!"

Madison knew that Paterson was not truly opposed to a new government. A crafty lawyer who had served as attorney general of New Jersey and who would one day sit on the U.S. Supreme Court, Paterson was an experienced negotiator. For the first two weeks of the convention he had remained silent, biding his time. Now he delivered a rhetorical right hook against the unsuspecting big-state delegates, pretending to object to *any* new Constitution. That way, he could "compromise" on a new Constitution that protected small states like New Jersey from being overpowered by large states like Virginia and Pennsylvania.

In fact, it wasn't long before Paterson tipped his hand. "Shall I," he asked rhetorically, "submit the welfare of the state of New Jersey, with five votes in the national council, opposed to Virginia who has sixteen votes?" According to Paterson, Virginia would be able to oppress New Jersey just as Britain had been able to oppress the American colonies. "Suppose, as it was in agitation before the war, that America had been represented in the British parliament and had sent two hundred members. What would this number avail against six hundred? We would have been as much enslaved in that case as when unrepresented—and, what is worse, without the prospect of redress!"

The comparison of Madison and his supporters to King George III and the British parliament was probably the most inflammatory language the convention had yet seen, but Paterson wasn't quite finished. "I therefore declare," he said, staring directly at James Madison, "that New Jersey will never confederate on the plan before the Committee. She would be swallowed up. I would rather submit to a monarch, to a despot, than to such a fate, and I shall not only oppose the plan here but, on my return home, do everything in my power to defeat it there!"[9]

Although Paterson's hyperbolic rhetoric took some of the delegates aback, the substance of his message was no surprise. Small states could not be expected to give up their disproportionate power without a fight, and if their delegates lost that fight at the convention, they would surely wage it in the ratification debates that would follow.

Six days later, Paterson formally presented an alternative to the Virginia Plan. In many ways, it was like Madison's, with new powers for Congress and provisions for executive and judiciary branches. But Paterson's New Jersey Plan included one seemingly nonnegotiable difference: Each state would enjoy equal representation in the legislature. One state. One vote.

The battle lines were now drawn.

And the convention's brief period of relative tranquility was history.

"Fatigue and Disgust"

The weeks after Paterson vowed to oppose the Virginia Plan were filled with threats, vitriol, insults, and an increasing likelihood that the small states and large states would never agree on a new constitution. Undoubtedly, the worst day—up to that point—was June 27, and the fault belonged to a thirty-nine-year-old, fifth-generation Maryland farmer named Luther Martin.

The convention had been scheduled to begin the day with a consideration of the question of Congress's legislative powers, but the delegates were anxious to continue the debate that Paterson had begun and that had hung like the sword of Damocles over the convention ever since—whether each state should have equal representation in Congress. After a vote to once again take up that matter, the broad-shouldered, sloppily dressed Martin stood to speak.

Because the delegates believed that every speaker should have the opportunity to make his case, none so much as considered interrupting Martin, even though he droned on in opposition to proportional representation for an entire afternoon. "An equal vote in each state," declared Martin in his gravelly voice, "was essential to the federal idea and was founded in justice and freedom, not merely in policy. Although the states may give up this right of sovereignty, they had not yet, and ought not!"

The hours-long monologue included interminable readings from Greek history, classical literature, political philosophy, and the common law. It was so long, was delivered with such incessant eagerness, and was filled with so many superlatives that it was difficult for any delegate to keep his focus on Martin's diatribe. Many of those delegates wondered whether Martin's penchant for liquor was partly to blame for his excited tone and the absence of any structure, but Martin was reckless by nature—with or without the influence of alcohol.

After three hours, Martin announced he was too exhausted to continue. For a moment the delegates breathed a sigh of relief—until Martin promised to pick up where he had left off first thing in the morning.

The next day, June 28, Martin delivered a speech that was, if possible, even more rambling and histrionic than the previous day's. The Virginia Plan was "ruinous and destructive." It was the equivalent of "slavery." And he "would rather see partial Confederacies"—disunion!—"than the plan on the table."

The day was half over before Martin's ramblings finally ended, and the speech had been a disaster for his cause. Even the small-state delegates who were likely to sympathize with him were alienated by his tirade. As he finished speaking, the Marylander saw, in a fellow delegate's words, nothing but "fatigue and disgust" from "whichever side of the house" he cast his "mortified eyes."[10]

Martin's refusal to surrender on equal representation was, however, no less uncompromising than James Madison's insistence on proportional representation, and after Martin concluded, Madison fired back with a scholarly analysis of the differences among the big states and the reasons why they would not unite to oppress the small states. He mentioned that the big states were divided on questions ranging from religion and culture to economic interests, and they had never in the nation's short history united against their smaller neighbors. His words were calmer and more impressive than Martin's, but his argument was no more effective. Neither side was yet willing to give an inch.

Lamenting the stalemate, the gout-ridden Ben Franklin rose in the afternoon with great effort to address the convention. "The small progress we have made after five weeks' close attendance and continual reasoning with each other," he said, "is methinks a melancholy proof of the imperfection of the human understanding." The delegates, Dr. Franklin explained, were "groping as it were in the dark to find political truth, and scarce able to distinguish it when presented to us."

Madison liked Franklin, but he wasn't sure where Franklin was going with this. The convention didn't need to be told that "small progress" had been made. And no one there had any doubt that his opponents were unable to see "political truth."

But Franklin had a surprise in store for them. "How has it happened," he asked, "that we have not hitherto once thought of humbly applying to the Father of Lights to illuminate our understandings?" After all, eleven years ago, the Continental Congress had "had daily prayer in this room for divine protection," and those prayers had been "heard" and "graciously answered."

Franklin explained, "I have lived, sir, a long time, and the longer I live, the more convincing proofs I see of this truth—that God governs in the affairs of men. And if a sparrow cannot fall to the ground without his notice, is it probable that an empire can rise without his aid?" Without the Lord's "concurring aid, we shall succeed in this political building no better than the Builders of Babel." Therefore, Franklin proposed beginning each day's deliberations with "prayers imploring the assistance of Heaven." His motion suggested "that one or more of the clergy of this city be requested to officiate."

In a different time and place, with less distrust and more tranquility, the men around Franklin would have endorsed his words and cheered his eloquence. But after three weeks of accusations, threats, and bitter gridlock, relations were so strained that the delegates could not even agree to pray together. Instead, the convention adjourned after another frustrating day that seemed to have pulled them even further apart. Compromise appeared unattainable, and, in at least a narrow sense, the convention didn't have a prayer.

"A Contest for *Power*, Not for Liberty"

The day after Franklin's foiled plea for "imploring the assistance of Heaven," the big-state delegates came out firing. Madison begged "the gentlemen representing the small states to renounce a principle which was confessedly unjust, which could *never* be admitted, and if admitted must infuse mortality into a Constitution which we wished to last forever." In a perhaps intentional pun on the failure of Franklin's previous proposal, he said, "I pray you to ponder well the consequences of suffering the Confederacy to go to pieces."

Madison's ally and future *Federalist Papers* coauthor, Alexander Hamilton, was more pointed. "It has been said that if the smaller states renounce their equality, they renounce at the same time their liberty." Hamilton paused, making sure that what he was about to say was unmistakable. "The truth is," he said, "it is a contest for *power*, not liberty."

The debate continued like that for some time, with each side accusing the other of being power hungry. After another Luther Martin harangue, mercifully shorter than his previous efforts, the future Supreme Court justice Oliver Ellsworth reminded the convention of a compromise previously proposed by his fellow Connecticut delegate, the socially awkward but often inexplicably persuasive Roger Sherman: proportional representation in the House; equal representation in the Senate.[11] Each state would have the same number of seats in the Senate, but the states with larger populations would have more representatives in the House. The compromise offered something for everyone, but it was as unacceptable to the large-state delegates now as it had been before. They had fought a revolution with the battle cry "No taxation without representation," and they would not consent to a legislative body that could raise the *taxes* in their states unless the allocation of seats in that body reflected the number of *people* in their states. The contest for power was far from over.

The next day, June's last Saturday, was a new low point for the convention in general and for James Madison in particular. In a speech that day, the Virginian predicted that the United States would be more politically divided between northern and southern states than between small and large states. It was a prescient point from a wise student of politics, but Madison then exacerbated animosities in the room by insulting the state of Connecticut.

Staring at Sherman and Ellsworth, Madison questioned Connecticut's commitment to the union by accusing the state of stinginess. "Did not Connecticut refuse her compliance to a federal requisition?" he asked. "Has she paid, for the last years, any money into the continental treasury? And does this look like government, or the observance of a solemn compact?"

By pointing out that Connecticut had not responded to Congress's request for more treasury funds, Madison hoped to demonstrate that "experience shows that the confederation is radically defective." But whatever the merits of Madison's critique of the state pushing hardest for a compromise, it was ill considered. Oliver Ellsworth quickly and angrily played the Revolutionary War card, pointing out that in that war, Connecticut "had more troops in the field than even Virginia." Its sacrifice had left Connecticut "greatly distressed and impoverished." Now, indebted due to her patriotism, "if she has proved delinquent through inability only, it is not more than others have been, without the same excuse."

Once again hoping to soothe tensions and appeal to nobler emotions, Ben Franklin made another effort to implore his colleagues to give an inch in order to get an inch. "When a broad table is to be made, and the edges of planks do not fit, the artist takes a little from both, and makes a good joint," said Franklin. "In like manner here, both sides must part with some of their demands in order that they may join in some accommodating proportion."

It was a nice sentiment.

It was immediately ignored.

Before long, Delaware's Gunning Bedford was in the midst of a speech even more pugnacious than Luther Martin's screed. He blasted the "ambition" and "avarice" of the big states before flatly telling Madison and his allies, "I do not, gentlemen, trust you."

It got worse. Bedford encouraged his small-state colleagues to stand firm against Madison, arguing that the big states would sooner compromise than break up the union. "The large states dare not dissolve the Confederation," he said. "If they do, the small ones will find some foreign ally of more honor and good faith, who will take them by the hand and do them justice."

In this very room, the Continental Congress had declared its independence from a foreign power. But now, at the nadir of the convention's deliberations, a delegate was threatening to ally his state with a foreign prince.

In truth, the immediate dissolution of the United States did not appear likely. But the immediate dissolution of the convention did. When George Mason wrote to the acting governor of Virginia that evening, he informed him that things "are now drawing to the point on which some of the fundamental principles must be decided, and two or three days will probably enable us to judge—which is at present very doubtful—whether any sound and effectual system can be established or not."

Dr. Franklin's Dinner Table

Delegates hoped that the Sabbath break for rest and worship might restore unity, but Monday, July 2, found the convention still stalemated. Early in the day, the large states voted down Connecticut's compromise of proportional representation in the House and equal representation in the Senate. In desperation, the convention created a "Grand Committee" to try to find a solution to the impasse. Each state would have one representative on the committee. If they couldn't find something more acceptable to more states than Connecticut's proposal, the convention would probably have to be dissolved, dooming the union to the instability and ineffectiveness of the Articles of Confederation. Praying that the committee could move them past the impasse the next day, the disappointed delegates broke for the evening.

Franklin was Pennsylvania's representative on the Grand Committee, and he figured that the best way to smooth the path to compromise would be to swap jokes and tell stories over a meal. The octogenarian bon vivant had employed the same trick on countless occasions in France, where his diplomatic skills had saved the revolution by allying France to the American cause. He knew the power of a little friendly hospitality.

Gathered in Franklin's dining room that evening, the small collection of delegates found the hospitable surroundings and good humor in stark contrast to the despair-inducing debates of the past three weeks. Franklin was a consummate host, having learned from the best—the French—how to throw a party. There was plenty of food and even more wine. And at the center of the evening was Franklin himself, full of jokes, tall tales, and the whimsically packaged wisdom of America's first and greatest Renaissance man.

There was something about Franklin that made everyone around him a little less edgy and a little more genial. If only for a few moments, the weary committee members let down their guards and forgot about their provincial prejudices. And tonight, if only for an evening, the delegates found that they actually enjoyed the company of the men they had been battling so bitterly. Whether their newfound camaraderie would make a difference in the next day's negotiations remained to be seen.

An Aging Optimist's Surprise

When the members of the Grand Committee convened by themselves in the assembly room of the statehouse the morning after their epic dinner, few knew what to expect. Some were tired from the late night at Franklin's. A few were hung over. But each was encouraged by last night's collegiality and the expectation that even if today didn't produce a compromise, it would at least be free of the vitriolic attacks that had plagued the convention in recent weeks.[12]

At least one of the men in the assembly room was optimistic: Benjamin Franklin. And although the other delegates might have been inclined to dismiss his optimism as the congenital disposition of an unwaveringly cheery man, today Franklin had a good reason for his high hopes. He had more to offer this committee than fine wine and good food. He also had a plan.

In the past, Franklin had suggested various plans for determining representation in Congress. His June 11 proposal had suggested funding Congress through a combination of mandatory and voluntary taxes. The mandatory taxes would affect each state equally and would be based on whatever amount the poorest state was willing to pay. The voluntary taxes would supplement whatever the compulsory taxes didn't cover.

Later in the month, Franklin had proposed equal representation in the Senate for some bills but representation tied to tax payments for laws about salaries, taxes, and appropriations. While this plan was more realistic than the last one, both proposals were complex and probably unworkable, and neither plan was deemed by the convention worthy of a vote or even a debate.

Franklin had learned from the tacit and total rejection of his previous proposals. He still believed there was room for a compromise that would appease the small states while avoiding the "taxation without representation" that the large states feared. But he now realized that any solution had to be simple.

After others on the Grand Committee began deliberations that morning with summaries of plans and counterplans long ago proposed and debated, Franklin put one hand on the arm of his chair, placed the other on the top of his cane, and pulled himself onto his gout-ridden feet. The long hair on the back of his balding head was already wet with sweat from the morning's summer heat. Eyeglasses rested on the tip of his nose. And from a face wrinkled by time and, perhaps, by the exuberances of a life lived to its fullest, his bright eyes peered into those of skeptical colleagues, who braced themselves for what they could only guess was another incomprehensible plan—or perhaps another call to prayer.

"The weaker states demand equal representation in at least one house," said Franklin slowly. This was, of course, not news to anyone in the assembly room. "I say, 'Let them have it,'" he said firmly. "There will be no constitution without it."

There were nods of agreement from Maryland's Luther Martin and New Jersey's William Paterson, as well as a few sighs from Virginia's George Mason and, in the chairman's seat, from Massachusetts's Elbridge Gerry.

"But the large states," continued Franklin, "reject a system that raises revenues for the treasury on a principle foreign to fair representation, do they not?" The committee members grumbled their assent, while Franklin added, "I say, 'Let them have what they wish too.'"

At this point Franklin could tell that the skepticism of the men around him was turning to impatience. The easy-to-like elder statesman might have had no enemies in the room, but he had no allies either. Not a single one of them had supported any of the proposals he had made at the convention. And not a single one expected him to say anything productive today.

"The solution is a House based on population and a Senate of equality in representation," Franklin said, as the big-state delegates groaned in exasperation. "But," said Franklin, raising his voice for the first time and smiling the grin of a chess player finding the path to checkmate, "all bills for raising money must originate in the House! That's the key! Equality in one house, but all taxes must come from the other house!"

Having finally shown the cards in his hands, Franklin smiled—and rightly so. The relieved expressions on his colleagues' faces told Franklin they liked what they heard. Gone were the looks of skepticism and irritation. Martin was sitting up straighter in his chair. Paterson's smile was almost as wide as Franklin's. And out of the corner of his eye Franklin could see Mason squinting, tilting his head, and looking at Gerry as if to say, *I think this could actually work. Right?*

The old Pennsylvanian proceeded to describe the proposal's advantages. It was a limit on the Senate found in most state constitutions, so it was already familiar to the public. It was something the small states could abide, since they would still be able to vote in the Senate against any tax increase introduced in the House. And it was just enough to alleviate the worst fears of some of the large states, which would not be subject to a dollar of taxes that did not originate in a legislative house based on the states' populations.

Believing his work completed, Franklin leaned against his cane and began the not-altogether-painless process of sitting down, but before he made it far, he stopped himself. He straightened his back and took the floor for one last thought. "For good measure," he said, "we might also bar the Senate from introducing laws respecting appropriations of money to be drawn out of the general treasury and for fixing the salaries of officers of the general government. And we will bar the Senate from amending such bills."

Some of the delegates were so surprised that Franklin had hit on such an ingenious idea that they were dumbfounded. Others were so happy at the prospect of a viable compromise that they wanted to applaud. But instead they did what they had come to Philadelphia to do: They talked some more.

The members of the committee examined the proposal from every angle. What would the rest of the convention think? What would the public think? How would it work in practice? They wanted to make sure there wasn't an even better compromise that they hadn't yet put their finger on.

There wasn't. Even though the proposal was really just a simplified version of Franklin's earlier idea of substituting a form of proportional representation for equal representation in the Senate on money bills, the simplicity of today's proposal, combined with its merits— coupled with the delegates' warm feelings after last night's dinner and their desperation to find some solution that would save the convention from dissolution—did the trick. Before the sun set on this eve of America's Independence Day, the new nation had a new compromise for what now appeared possible: a new constitution.

When Massachusetts's Elbridge Gerry introduced the compromise proposal to the full convention after the July 4 holiday, he made clear that the committee had endorsed it not because everyone believed it was perfect but because everyone could live with it. "The committee were of different opinions," he said, "and agreed to the report merely in order that some ground of accommodation might be proposed."

Then, on July 16, after nearly two weeks of debate about how slaves would affect proportional representation in the House—a foreshadowing of the nation's North-South divide and a small vindication of Madison's prediction that the country's deepest divisions would be geographic—the convention voted on the Grand Committee's proposal that money bills must originate in the House of Representatives.

After a month of acrimonious arguments and repeated rejections of various compromises, the convention walked itself back from the brink of catastrophe.

Franklin's proposal passed—by just a single state's vote.

The Constitution Is Born

Several weeks after Franklin's "origination clause" was adopted, there was a last-ditch effort by an unlikely alliance of individual delegates to remove it. Delegates from the small states saw a chance to extract one last concession from the large states, and a few of the big-state delegates worried that the clause would undermine the Senate's independence from the House.

South Carolina's Charles Pinckney was the first to move to strike the clause, and Virginia's George Mason quickly rose, with irritation, to fight the motion. "I am unwilling to travel over this ground again," said Mason, who had served on the select committee that created the clause. "To strike out the section is to unhinge the compromise."

That compromise had been long in coming, and it had rescued the convention from failure at the last possible moment. Moreover, Mason believed the Senate would be viewed as "an aristocratic body" less representative of the people than the House, and thus "the purse strings should never be put into its hands."

Mason's two arguments—that the convention's compromise on representation had depended on the origination clause and that the clause guarded against taxation without representation—became the battle cry for the clause's defenders. But in his desire not "to travel over this ground again," he was to be sorely disappointed.

On multiple days in August, the delegates battled over the origination clause. Parting ways with his fellow South Carolinian Charles Pinckney, Pierce Butler was "for adhering to the principle which had been settled."[13] Oliver Ellsworth reminded the convention that the clause was "of consequence by some members from the larger states."[14] Edmund Randolph tried to "remind the members from the smaller states of the compromise by which the larger states were entitled to this privilege."[15]

Every time an opponent of the clause spoke up, its supporters fired back. "Taxation and representation are strongly associated in the minds of the people," argued Elbridge Gerry, "and they will not agree that any but their immediate representatives shall meddle with their purses." He believed that, if the Constitution lacked an origination clause, the people would probably not ratify it: "The acceptance of the plan will inevitably fail, if the Senate be not restrained from originating money bills."

Ratification was on the mind of each delegate at the convention. The delegates knew that even if the convention agreed on a Constitution, its fate would depend on whether the American people agreed to accept it. After the convention in Philadelphia ended (assuming its delegates agreed on a Constitution), every state would hold its own convention, where representatives of the people would debate the merits of the proposed Constitution. Only if the states' conventions voted to ratify it would the Constitution become the nation's supreme law. If enough state conventions voted against it, then the Articles of Confederation would remain in effect.

Many others agreed with Gerry that ratification depended on Franklin's origination clause. Delaware's John Dickinson argued that "all the prejudices of the people would be offended by refusing this exclusive privilege to the House of Representatives." Right on his heels was Randolph, urging the delegates to realize that "this point is of such consequence" that on it depended "the peace of this country."

In the end, the origination clause survived—barely. On several occasions the coalition against it managed to remove the clause altogether. But at the Constitutional Convention no vote was final until the Constitution was signed, and the clause's supporters succeeded in putting back into the nation's charter a modified version of Franklin's proposal.

Under the final language of the clause, the Senate could amend any law, and the House was no longer the sole body able to originate bills related to spending and federal salaries. But it *was* the sole body able to originate tax bills. When the Constitution was signed, it provided: "All bills for raising Revenue shall originate in the House of Representatives; but the Senate may propose or concur with Amendments as on other Bills."

The compromise that saved the Constitution, for which James Madison had waited so long, had survived into September.

That compromise would survive the contentious ratification process of the next ten months.[16]

But it would not survive into the twenty-first century.

"We Love You, Obama!"

Just short of eight months since the new president had taken his oath of office, this Thursday in mid-September appeared to be another typical day in the extraordinarily ambitious presidency of Barack Obama.

At a late-morning pep rally in College Park, Maryland, just ten miles from the White House, the president was in fine form. He had come to speak about health insurance reform—or, as he called it, a "defining struggle of this generation."

The president faced widespread opposition to his plan to move toward a socialized health-care system—not just from Republicans but also from a few Democrats. Some Democrats planned to vote against the law. Others were negotiating to trade their votes for promises of hundreds of millions of dollars in Medicaid funding for their states. The law's passage depended on the Obama administration's twisting a lot of arms and making deals with Democratic lawmakers and unions that raised some serious ethical and constitutional questions.

Despite the opposition to his plan, the president left little doubt that he intended to win the struggle for a law that would require Americans to obtain health insurance, regulate insurers, vastly expand government-funded insurance, and pay for trillions in new spending over the next decades with a formidable host of new taxes. His legacy depended on it. And he would do just about anything to prevail.

His College Park audience didn't need much convincing of the benefits of the president's plan. The White House had staged the event like a campaign rally and had tried to make sure that only true believers were in the audience.

"We love you, Obama!" one person called out, interrupting the president's platitudes.[17]

"I love you too!" he shouted back, unmatched in his talents as cheerleader in chief.

"It has now been nearly a century since Teddy Roosevelt first called for health-care reform," said Obama. "It's been attempted by nearly every president and every Congress since. And our failure to get it done—year after year, and decade after decade—has placed a burden on families and on businesses and on taxpayers that we can no longer sustain. So I may not be the first president to take up the cause of health-care reform; I am determined to be the last, with your help!"

After making a few promises he couldn't keep—such as his vow that "if you already have health insurance, nothing in this plan will require you to change what you have"—the president shifted gears. He told a long story about a campaign stop in rural South Carolina. Describing a woman who started a back-and-forth chant with the catchphrases "Fired up!" and "Ready to go!" he asked his audience, "So I want to know—are you fired up?"

"Fired up!" they called back, applauding their hero.

"Ready to go?" he shouted.

"Ready to go!" they shouted back.

"Fired up?"

"Fired up!!"

"Ready to go?"

"Ready to go!!"

The cheering crowd was loving this.

"Fired up?"

"Fired up!!!"

"Ready to go?" he asked one last time.

"Ready to go!!!" they screamed back.

The room was electric. The applause was infectious. The president was basking in his fans' adulation like the Beatles arriving in America. The audience acted like the future was theirs for the taking.

At that point the president of the United States could have asked his army of acolytes to do anything. Turn back the tide of the oceans? No problem. Create world peace? Easy as pie. So for his final line, he didn't ask them to *merely* help him change the way Americans paid their doctors. No. The world was their oyster, and nothing could stop them from imposing their will. So with the crowd "fired up" and "ready to go," Barack Obama ended with the most ambitious call to action he could think of.

"Let's go change the world!"

Absent from the president's nearly thirty-minute speech was any explanation of how his plans to "change the world" were constitutional. There was, in fact, no indication by the new president of any legal limits on any federal power to issue mandates on individuals or enlist state governments in this cause.

Nor was there any reason why any observer should have been surprised by that glaring omission. After all, these world changers were "fired up." They were "ready to go." And it turned out that they could not be bothered by the quaint relics of history—not even the one signed exactly 222 years earlier on that very day, a day others around the nation were celebrating as Constitution Day.

The Unlikely Origins of the Patient Protection and Affordable Care Act

On that same Constitution Day, back on Capitol Hill, Representative Charlie Rangel introduced House Resolution 3590 in Congress. The obscure bill was titled the Service Members Home Ownership Tax Act of 2009. It sought to "amend the Internal Revenue Code of 1986 to modify the first-time homebuyers credit in the case of members of the Armed Forces and certain other Federal employees."[18]

It had none of the glitz of the president's speech, and it had nothing whatsoever to do with health-insurance reform.

Not yet.

But although no one realized it at the time, this uncontroversial bill would soon become the vehicle chosen by the president and his congressional allies to sidestep the Constitution they had sworn to protect.

Less than a month after the president's rally in College Park, the House of Representatives voted on House Resolution 3590. Tax incentives for service members were far from controversial, and the bill passed with 416 votes. Not a single representative opposed it.

A few weeks later, Nevada's Harry Reid was in a bind. As leader of the Democratic majority in the Senate, he wanted nothing more than to pass President Obama's health-insurance reform. He needed to introduce the reform bill that had been crafted in committee, and he needed to do it as soon as possible. But the bill had at least seventeen different tax provisions, and, thanks to Ben Franklin, the Constitution bars the Senate from originating tax laws. "All bills for raising Revenue shall originate in the House of Representatives," says the first line of Article I, Section 7.

The founders had used the origination clause to ensure that taxation would originate only in the house most representative of, and accountable to, the people. In the *Federalist Papers* (*Federalist 58*), James Madison had written, "The house of representatives cannot only refuse, but they alone can propose the supplies requisite for the support of government." As Madison said of the people's most direct representatives within the federal government, they "hold the purse," which "may in fact be regarded as the most complete and effectual weapon with which any constitution can arm the immediate representatives of the people, for obtaining a redress of every grievance, and for carrying into effect every just and salutary measure."

But when then–Majority Leader Harry Reid walked into the Senate chamber on November 21, 2009, he didn't seem overly concerned about the origination clause's purpose. He had taxes to raise.

He wanted them passed. And he didn't seem very concerned about how he did it.

That's where House Resolution 3590 came into play. Reid proposed a simple amendment: Strike all the language from House Resolution 3590, and replace it with the president's health-insurance plan. Voilà: a health-care reform bill inside a tax bill that, at least in a very technical sense, "originated" in the House.

Of course, if Reid's "amendment" could satisfy the origination clause, the clause was pointless. It provided no restraint whatsoever on the Senate. It provided no protection against the taxation the founding generation so feared. In other words, if Reid was *right*, then the compromise that saved the Constitution was *wrong*.

This flagrant disregard for the Constitution was momentous. Congress had been ignoring the origination clause for decades, but never with a law as far-reaching as Obamacare. The language Reid put into H.R. 3590 tacked onto our nation's $18 trillion debt an $800 billion expansion of Medicaid. It made medical costs higher by taxing medical devices that save lives and prevent illnesses. It eliminated affordable health-insurance plans that Americans preferred to keep and led to higher, burdensome premiums on new plans they didn't want. It penalized employers that grow jobs by expanding their workforce, and it threatened workers' take-home pay by incentivizing employers to cut workers' hours. It raised taxes by $500 billion and empowered an already-politicized Internal Revenue Service to play a major role in American health care. It trampled on the freedom of religious employers and hospitals by forcing them to provide free birth control in violation of their religious beliefs. And—through its individual mandate—it transformed the federal government into an institution that can force you to buy anything a bureaucrat in Washington decides you need.

After Harry Reid's attack on the origination clause, H.R. 3590 emerged with a new title: the Patient Protection and Affordable

Care Act. But Americans, of course, know it by its more accurate—and less Orwellian—name: Obamacare.

For several years after the law's passage, Obamacare's assault on the notion that ours is a federal government of limited powers was litigated in courts from coast to coast. Even today, many of those challenges are continuing. And conservatives in Congress are still fighting to repeal Obamacare and replace it with constitutionally permissible reforms that actually accomplish what the law's technical title proposes: improving patients' care and reducing patients' costs.

If only Harry Reid and Barack Obama had been faithful to the origination clause, none of those lawsuits and legislative battles would have been necessary. No one in America would be losing a popular health-insurance plan that a Washington bureaucrat has outlawed. The economy would be stronger. Taxes would be lower. Health care would be better.

Today, Obamacare exists because of a few politicians who chose to protect and defend their own interests and ideologies instead of the Constitution of the United States of America.

CHAPTER 3

From Congress to a King

THE FORGOTTEN LEGISLATIVE
POWERS CLAUSE

> *All legislative Powers herein granted shall be vested in*
> *a Congress of the United States, which shall consist of a*
> *Senate and House of Representatives.*
>
> —UNITED STATES CONSTITUTION, ARTICLE I, SECTION 1

AT THE CLOSE OF THE CONSTITUTIONAL CONVENTION, WHEN
an elderly Benjamin Franklin hobbled out of the hall where delegates had debated the fate of the young nation for the length of the hottest Philadelphia summer in thirty-seven years, he was asked by a curious bystander, "Well, Doctor, what have we got—a republic or a monarchy?"

"A republic," Franklin famously replied, "if you can keep it."

The bystander's question was a fair one, especially given that in 1787 monarchs held power in almost every corner of the world. King Louis XVI still reigned in France. King Carlos IV ruled Spain—and most of South America. Queen Maria sat on the throne of Portugal, and King Frederick Wilhelm III wore the crown of Prussia. Czarina Catherine the Great had recently expanded Russia's borders at the expense of the Ottoman Empire, which was led by Sultan Abdülhamid I. Shogun Tokugawa Ienari presided over Japan, and in China the Qianlong Emperor was fifty-one years into his sixty-one-year reign. Meanwhile, in London, King George III was not yet halfway through his six decades on the throne of the United Kingdom.[1]

America was unique. Its soldiers had fought from Lexington to Yorktown to defend their homes and their rights against monarchy. Its citizens were governed by state legislatures, elected governors, and representatives in Congress. And its most basic creed held that individuals should be subject only to the rules of lawmakers chosen by the people.

So it was no surprise that the government designed during that Philadelphia summer in 1787 would be ruled not by a prince but by the people—"We the People" would be in charge. Radical as it was—on *every other continent* in the world—to propose that men could govern themselves, it was, in the United States, almost taken for granted. The issue in doubt was not, as Franklin's questioner asked, whether the convention's delegates would create a republic. The real question, as Franklin noted, was whether they could design one that would endure.

The convention's delegates had been sent to Philadelphia to do exactly that, and at the heart of their design was Congress. That's why the first section of the Constitution's first article provides that "All legislative Powers herein granted shall be vested in a Congress of the United States, which shall consist of a Senate and House of Representatives." That simple sentence captures, more than any other, the audacity of the American experiment and its break with millennia of pharaohs, despots, and divinely inspired potentates. It was no accident that the framers made it first in the structure of the new Constitution; they saw it as first in importance to the new republic.

The founders did not take their task lightly. Their revolutionary experiment in self-government might, they had to admit, not work. But it was worth the gamble because the alternatives were too terrible to contemplate. Freedom itself depended on an elected legislature of citizen lawmakers who would be accountable—directly in the House, indirectly in the Senate—to the people. They understood that "We the People" would never truly be free unless we retained control over the branch of government responsible for making laws. It was not enough that *some* of this legislative power be vested in a Congress whose members would stand accountable to the people at regular intervals. It was necessary to give Congress *all* legislative powers.

Of course, the Constitution also created an executive and a judiciary, but its drafters understood that keeping Congress's powers separate from the other branches was necessary to preserve liberty. In the *Federalist Papers*, James Madison wrote that "no political truth is certainly of greater intrinsic value, or is stamped with the authority of more enlightened patrons of liberty" than the maxim that "the legislative, executive, and judiciary departments ought to be separate and distinct." Liberty cannot long survive in a nation where the person or entity that *enforces* the laws is the same person or entity that *writes* the laws.

That ideal of separated powers, however, is far from the reality in which we live. The first line of the first article of the Constitution has become so distorted by successive Supreme Courts, Congresses, and power-hungry presidents that most laws are now written and promulgated by executive agencies, not by Congress. It is a system that is not just ripe for abuse but already being abused. Our federal regulatory system heavily burdens families, consumers, workers, small business owners, and vital American institutions, all of which are adversely affected by arbitrary regulations produced by unaccountable bureaucrats at the EPA, the NLRB, the FCC, the SEC, and a host of other federal agencies that exercise rule-making authority largely unchecked by Congress and the courts. They echo one of the complaints against King George III, as articulated in the Declaration of Independence, which condemned the despised monarch for erecting "a multitude of New Offices" and sending "hither swarms of Officers to harass our people, and eat out their substance."

For nearly a century Washington has been sapping Congress of the legislative powers guaranteed by the first line of Article I and creating what Madison warned against: "a gradual concentration of the several powers in the same department." This chapter tells the story of how we got here—including the Constitutional Convention's resounding rejection of the brilliant but misguided Alexander Hamilton's proposal for an American king and ending with shortsighted choices by Congress, the courts, and even the citizenry that have combined to undermine the first article of the Constitution and produce something very much like a monarchy.

Lessons from a Lynch Mob

On the evening of May 10, 1775, Alexander Hamilton was roused from his bedroom by calls for help from his friend Nicholas Ogden. A mob of unruly Patriots was on its way to King's College to attack the school's Tory president, Myles Cooper.

An alumnus of King's College, Ogden didn't want to see his alma mater's president tarred and feathered by the Sons of Liberty. Having already warned Cooper, he was now raising the alarm in the rooms around Cooper's residence. In an instant Hamilton was out of his bed and—much to the surprise of his roommate Robert Troup—ready to help.

Hamilton was no friend to Cooper. In recent months, Hamilton and the college president had sparred in the pages of New York's newspapers. The city had no fiercer defender of the crown than Dr.

Myles Cooper. And it had no more eloquent advocate of liberty than Alexander Hamilton.

But now a mob was attempting to torture—or worse—an innocent man. That was no way, Hamilton believed, to defend liberty.

When Hamilton got a notion of right and wrong stuck in his head, he couldn't be reasoned with. The mob would number in the hundreds, and he would be alone in standing between them and Myles Cooper. But Hamilton knew the difference between honor and dishonor. And he had made his choice long ago.

That Patriot Alexander Hamilton would stand on Myles Cooper's steps, defending a Tory against a violent (and violently drunk) mob, was just one of the ironies that had defined his twenty years. Born in St. Croix, far from the American colonies, he was now an eloquent pamphleteer for the cause of American liberties. Barred from attending the Church of England's elementary school because he was the illegitimate son of a single mother, he was now, thanks to sponsors' beneficence after his mother's death, a student at King's College—soon to be renamed Columbia. With no military experience, he had formed a Patriot artillery unit, drilling by day and studying by night. But none of those contradictions was as stark or immediate as the courageously stubborn stand he was taking in defense of his political enemy.

"Come out or we'll burn you out!" shouted an intoxicated, torch-carrying man at the front of the mob. Others carrying clubs chimed in with "Die, Tory!"[2]

Hamilton could smell the hot tar. He had seen the depths of man's depravity when he had witnessed slaves beaten and whipped on the sugar plantations of St. Croix. This wasn't the first time he had seen that, left to their own devices, men could be ugly creatures.

Standing on the steps of the building, Hamilton shouted to the men to pause and consider their actions.

But the mob was not in a reflective mood. These men had spent the month since Lexington and Concord robbing British ships, parading through town like drunken hooligans, and burning Tories in effigy. Tonight they had torn down the gate to Cooper's house, and the fire in their eyes made it quite clear that nothing would satisfy them more than tearing Cooper limb from limb.

Hamilton didn't expect to be able to reason with the mob. Men like these were no better than animals, incapable of acting with rational restraint. But if he could stall them long enough, Myles Cooper could escape out the back door. And so Alexander Hamilton began the first great political lecture of his life.

"Consider your cause and the injury you inflict on it," shouted Hamilton over the taunts and threats of the mob, displaying to the largest audience of his young life all the confidence, courage, and contempt for democratic disorder that would propel and plague him at every stage of his soon-to-be-illustrious service to his adopted country. "With your conduct," he scolded, "you disgrace and injure the glorious cause of liberty."[3]

As Hamilton launched his final insult, he congratulated himself on a job well done. He had filibustered long enough for Dr. Cooper to escape over the back fence. Cooper was now racing toward the wharf, where he would find deliverance through a British ship soon to sail for England. It was now time to let the mob have its way with the college president's quarters—and to return to his own.

"Well," said Robert Troup once Hamilton made it back to the safety of their room, "I see you survived. That must mean Dr. Cooper has survived as well?"

Nodding, his voice hoarse from shouting, Alexander Hamilton whispered, "They're an ugly, unreasonable lot, Robert."

"The mob?" asked Troup.

"The people," replied Hamilton.

"An Executive for Life"

On June 18, 1787, twelve years later, Alexander Hamilton rose and surveyed the East Room of the Pennsylvania State House—a red brick building better known in later years as Independence Hall. On any given day sat some thirty of the Constitutional Convention's fifty-five delegates, the remainder commuting back and forth to handle business in their states. Those before Hamilton included allies and adversaries, but he doubted whether even his closest friends were prepared for the speech he was about to deliver.

"To deliver my sentiments on so important a subject," began Hamilton, "when the first characters in the union have gone before me, inspires me with the greatest diffidence, especially when my own ideas are so materially dissimilar to the plans now before the committee." Had he begun by merely feigning humility, or was he providing a real reason why he had sat silent for the first three weeks of the convention, listening to older men debate the future of the infant nation? No matter. By the end of his first sentence, Hamilton had come to his point: His "own ideas" were "materially dissimilar" to theirs, and he was ready to have his say. "My situation is disagreeable," he added by way of a further warning, "but it would be criminal not to come forward on a question of such magnitude."[4]

Behind the desks sat delegates who were almost invariably better born than Alexander Hamilton—and, whether because of that fact or in spite of it, almost invariably more trusting of "the people." They had disagreements about whether state legislatures should be *slightly* more powerful than a federal government or *vastly* more powerful than it, but each of them believed with an almost religious ferocity in local, republican government by the people.

Hamilton looked across the hall to the Virginia delegation, where General George Washington sat straight as a board—always there, always silent, always saying with his gravitas and reputation that history would remember these men. It would record their triumph. Or their failure.

And what did General Washington see in the respected attorney from New York speaking before him? A former aide-de-camp who had been more valuable to him than any other soldier in the Continental Army. A bright mind that bordered on genius, with a self-confidence that often bordered on arrogance. Five feet, seven inches. Brilliant blue eyes. Red hair. Powdered cheeks. A lean man, but far from frail. Sometimes uncomfortably candid but generally well mannered. He could be unusually formal and overly vain, but almost always charming, at least until the subject turned to politics.

"I have well considered the subject," explained Hamilton, "and I have great doubts whether a national government on the Virginia Plan can be made effectual." He was rejecting Madison's design for a strong national government divided among three branches. But unlike the Virginia Plan's other critics, Hamilton wasn't arguing for a more modest proposal. "The British government is the best in the world," he declared, "and I doubt much whether anything short of it will do in America."

There was a collective gasp from Hamilton's small audience. Americans had bled and died for freedom from Great Britain. Hamilton himself had led the charge that broke the British lines at Yorktown. In the minds of the men around Hamilton, they had rebelled not just against *the* king but against the notion of *any* king.

Hoping to hang on to his audience, Hamilton quickly said, "I hope gentlemen of different opinions will bear with me in this." Those "gentlemen," Hamilton believed, didn't comprehend the extent of America's problems. Congress was out of money and unable to raise more. States had erected countless barriers to trade across borders. Setting a foreign policy was impossible. And in places like western Massachusetts, the organs of state government had been toppled by mob rule, as debtors rebelled against creditors by closing down courthouses. The "gentlemen of different opinions" didn't know how dangerous ungoverned men could be.

"Great Britain," Hamilton unapologetically proclaimed, "is the only government in the world which unites public strength with individual security." And Hamilton was determined to explain to them why, especially when it came to the executive branch, "the English model is the only good one on this subject."

To defend "the English model," Hamilton thoroughly reviewed the defects of every other system of government tried or imagined by man. The models of the ancient Greeks—Athens, Lacedaemon, Thebes, Phocis, and Macedonia. Rome and Carthage. Charlemagne's court. The Hanseatic League, the German Diet, the Swiss cantons, and the Polish Commonwealth. Though Hamilton was capable of lightness and charm, especially around ladies, his speech could turn didactic and professorial when he determined to get to the bottom of a debated subject. At such times there was, in the words of a contemporary, "no skimming over the surface of a subject with him."⁵

Woven implicitly and explicitly throughout Hamilton's tour through the history of Western civilization was a comparison between the defects of failed states and the defects of the Articles of Confederation, which included omissions of an executive, a judiciary, an effective means to raise revenues, and the power to enact laws that were directly binding on individual citizens. As a result of the federal government's deficiencies, the American republic was currently in shambles. "Our job is to make independence work, but what a terrible situation we're in," Hamilton had written to a friend. "I've a powerful remedy for this problem—strong government—but if not taken quickly, the patient will die."⁶

More than halfway into what would become an uninterrupted six-hour speech, Hamilton turned from history and a diagnosis of the problem to his proposed solution of "strong government." At the head of that government should be "an elected monarch."

And there it was. The dreaded word. *Monarch.* Even the face of Hamilton's friend, James Madison, turned ashen. Madison was the convention's most vital defender of a profoundly expanded federal government, but he knew that associating an expanded government with a king would not bring new supporters to his cause. At best, this speech would only damage Hamilton's reputation and future. At worst, it would irreparably doom Madison's vision of a reformed and robust national government.

Still, Hamilton plowed ahead. To speak this truth, as he saw it, to many of the most respected minds of his country, Hamilton had to call upon a special combination of uncompromising stubbornness and unabashed disdain for the "popular passions" of his fellow Americans. But it also required a reckless courage. Hamilton knew how unpopular his ideas were. He understood that giving voice to them would provide invaluable ammunition to his political enemies for the rest of his life. But he also believed that America needed to be saved from itself. It needed a strong executive. A king. A father.

"An executive for life has not," explained Hamilton, "motive for forgetting his fidelity, and will therefore be a safer depositary of power." A king would not succumb to public hysteria or bend to political motivations in order to win an election, he reasoned. Hamilton was aware that his ideas were unpopular, but he was determined to make them see what he believed—that the union would soon dissolve unless the convention voted to create a leader able to resist the kinds of ugly passions and prejudices that had once led a mob to try to tar and feather the head of Hamilton's college.

After six hours of speaking, Hamilton closed by admitting once again that his plan was "very remote from the idea of the people." But "the people," he promised, "are gradually ripening in their opinions of government. They begin to be tired of an excess of democracy." Throwing in a culinary metaphor, he argued that the people would be best served by the hearty beef of a strong government, not the cheap and mild pork of the Articles of Confederation. "And what is the Virginia Plan," he asked, "but pork still, with a little change of the sauce?"

As he sat down, there was the briefest of barely polite applause, followed by total silence. No one laughed at Hamilton's attempt to conclude with a bit of humor. No one offered any support. The delegates appeared weary and all-too-ready to return to their boarding rooms.

It was an awkward end to the most extraordinary speech of the Constitutional Convention. Hamilton had gone "all in," not only for a strong central government but for one led by an elected king. He had asked his skeptical audience to bear with him for six hours, and, in a testament to their civility, not one of them had interrupted him. But the expressions on their faces did not augur well.

The kindest reaction Hamilton received was from Benjamin Franklin. He was asleep. In contrast, Hamilton's ally James Madison was alert—but with worry in his eyes and woe written across his face.[7]

Hamilton's fellow New York delegates, Robert Yates and John Lansing, looked bemused. Fierce defenders of state sovereignty and opponents of any centralized government, they had known that Hamilton believed in the kind of government he proposed, but they had figured he wouldn't be foolish enough to admit it. They knew that the day's fireworks could only help them by inflaming the fears of fence-sitting delegates who worried that replacing the Articles of Confederation with a new constitution would lead to a tyrannical federal government.

Mercifully, a motion to adjourn for the day broke the silence that followed Hamilton's conclusion. It was quickly seconded and adopted, and the shocked delegates slowly made their way out of the hall.

As the delegates filed past him and headed to the City Tavern and

Indian Queen for drinks and dinner, Hamilton slumped in his chair. He was mentally exhausted from the intense and prolonged effort he had put into his speech. He was physically spent after six hours on his feet. And he was emotionally drained by weeks of fretting about the fate of the country he'd been fighting for since he was twenty years old.

After the last delegate exited the East Room, Hamilton looked around the chamber where American independence had been debated and declared nearly eleven years earlier. He thought back to his service at that time on General Washington's war council. He had loved the feeling of camaraderie that came from being a part of George Washington's military family. Since then, the orphan had established a family of his own. But now, with no one left in the East Room and with the memory of his fellow delegates' expressions of bemusement and disgust, Hamilton felt, in more ways than one, alone.

"All Legislative Powers Herein Granted Shall Be Vested in a Congress"

Hamilton hadn't expected his marathon address to be met with immediate applause or overwhelming support, but he had hoped that the next day the delegates would at least use it as an opportunity to explore the possibility of a strong central government led by an elected monarch.

They didn't.

In a testament to their belief that men are able to govern themselves; that Congress should be the strongest branch of the government; and that a government of limited powers provides the best protection of individual liberty, the delegates were so dismissive of Hamilton's proposal that they declined even to debate it.

Instead, James Madison rose on the morning after Hamilton's

speech to try to undo the damage the New Yorker had inflicted on his cause. Madison wanted to make crystal clear to the convention delegates that a vote for a new constitution would *not* be a vote in favor of either Alexander Hamilton or his reckless plan to create an American despot.

Even though Madison was only thirty-six years old, no one in the room was more respected for his intellectual acumen. A scholarly bachelor, Madison had won the admiration of his colleagues not with charm or charisma but by the depths of his knowledge of history and political philosophy, as well as the courage he had shown two years earlier when he fought Patrick Henry, the most popular politician in his home state, in an effort to advance religious freedom in Virginia.

Without breathing a word about Hamilton's plan, Madison used his address this June morning to return the conversation to the two other plans that had been presented: Madison's "Virginia Plan" and William Paterson's "New Jersey Plan."

Madison conceded that no plan was perfect, but in an address later remembered as his finest hour, the young Virginian emphasized the necessity of compromise. "I beg you," he said softly to skeptics of the Virginia Plan, "to consider the situation in which you would remain in case your pertinacious adherence to an inadmissible plan should prevent the adoption of any plan." In other words, if every delegate stubbornly clung to his first preference for a constitutional order, no plan would garner sufficient support. "The contemplation of such an event is painful."

There was one aspect of the Virginia and New Jersey plans that was, however, nonnegotiable: America could not have a king. Neither plan contemplated an unaccountable executive who would serve for life. And like the New Jersey Plan, the Virginia Plan put at the center of the federal government an elected Congress. It provided that "the national Legislature ought to consist of Two Branches"; that "the members of the first branch of the national Legislature ought to be elected by the People of the several States for the term of three years"; that "the members of the second Branch of the national Legislature ought to be chosen by the individual Legislatures" of the states; and that "each branch ought to possess the right of originating acts."[8]

When Madison finished speaking, the convention voted in favor of proceeding to consider the Virginia Plan over the New Jersey Plan, with the understanding that every line of Madison's plan was still subject to discussion and amendment. At each session for the next ninety days, they debated every imaginable aspect of republican government, but Madison's plan for a Congress consisting of two houses received no significant opposition. In mid-September, when Gouverneur Morris's Committee on Style produced a final draft for the convention to vote up or down, the first article of the new constitution began, "All legislative Powers herein granted shall be vested in a Congress of the United States, which shall consist of a Senate and House of Representatives."

In the United States of America, laws would be made by a Congress, not a king.

A World Not Far from That Imagined by Hamilton

In the seventeen years after the Constitutional Convention, up until the moment when Aaron Burr's lead shot found Alexander Hamilton on the bluffs of Weehawken, Hamilton's enemies whispered rumors about the proposal he had made in Philadelphia. *Did you hear he wanted a king? Elected or hereditary? With limited or unlimited powers?* Even if Hamilton had survived his duel in Weehawken, this leader of the Federalist Party would never and *could* never have been elected president. All because of one foolish speech—and the toxic slur that followed him after it: *monarchist.*

And yet, in many ways, we are living in a world not entirely unlike that of Hamilton's imagination. The story of how we went from the government created by our Constitution to a kind of government that was repugnant to the founders in Philadelphia—who did not even deem Hamilton's proposal fit for debate—is as little understood as it is dangerous to American democracy.

It is a story that begins with an economic depression, a landslide election, and a New Deal.

Roosevelt's Inaugural Address

On March 4, 1933, Franklin D. Roosevelt surveyed the thousands of cheering Americans standing before the East Portico of the U.S. Capitol. He listened to a rousing rendition of "Hail to the Chief" and basked in the adulation of a public that had awarded him 89 percent of their electoral votes. When the appointed hour arrived, the newly elected president, standing tall and straight despite the polio that crippled his legs, swore to "preserve, protect, and defend the Constitution of the United States."

The problems facing the nation's thirty-second president were as daunting as any faced since Abraham Lincoln had first sworn the same oath on that same spot. The price of goods had, in President Roosevelt's words, "shrunken to fantastic levels." Taxes were high, but government was "faced by serious curtailment of income." Trade was "frozen." Industry's "withered leaves" lay dormant. Farmers could "find no markets for their produce." Families' savings had vanished. And "a host of unemployed citizens" struggled to survive while "an equally great number" saw "little return" for their labor.[9]

Half a world away, economic chaos was leading to fascism and desperation in Europe. In America many feared that the nation's economic depression meant that the collapse of the American experiment was not far behind.

But Franklin Roosevelt rejected that dire view. "This great nation," he declared, in his unmistakable accent and with his unshakable optimism, "will endure as it has endured, will revive, and will prosper." Just one minute into his inaugural address, the new president reassured Americans with his "firm belief that the only thing we have to fear is fear itself."

For good reason, generations of American schoolchildren would memorize and repeat that now-famous line. But its words were hardly the most important ones the president would proclaim. Far more critical to the American republic than Roosevelt's rejection of fear was the *substance* of his plan to defeat the Depression, explained by the now largely forgotten remainder of the address.

President Roosevelt believed the Depression should be treated "as we would treat the emergency of a war." A return to economic stability depended on "a trained and loyal army willing to sacrifice for the good of a common discipline." Americans must be "ready and willing to submit our lives and property to such discipline" and accept this "sacred obligation with a unity of duty hitherto evoked only in time of armed strife."

What instruments of "war" did the president imagine? The government would need to engage "on a national scale in a redistribution"; "to provide a better use of land for those best fitted for the land"; "to raise the values of agricultural products"; and to adopt "national planning for and supervision of all forms of transportation and of communications and other utilities which have a definitely public character," as well as "supervision of all banking and credits and investments." There was hardly any element of economic life in America that would be outside the domain of federal regulation.

Most of these initiatives represented a fundamental transformation in the relationship between the people and their federal government. Never before had our national leaders assumed the power to regulate private land, market prices, and every major industry in the country.

Toward the end of the inaugural address, the president doubled down. He explained that these initiatives might also transform the relationship between Congress and the president. "It is hoped that the normal balance of executive and legislative authority may be wholly adequate to meet the unprecedented task before us," he said. "But it may be that an unprecedented demand and need for undelayed action may call for temporary departure from that normal balance of public procedure."

It was an audacious proclamation. Franklin Roosevelt not only expected the government to make new rules for almost every aspect of economic life in America; he expected the executive branch to make those rules. He completely ignored the risk, that, in the words of the founders' greatest influence, Charles de Montesquieu, "when legislative power is united with executive power in a single person or in a single body of the magistracy, there is no liberty, because one can fear that the same monarch or senate that makes tyrannical laws will execute them tyrannically."[10] He entirely abandoned the principle that, in John Locke's words, a legislature "cannot transfer the power of making laws to any other hands, for it being but a delegated power from the people, they who have it cannot pass it over to others." From that moment on, if Franklin Roosevelt had his way, the president would do what Congress had always done: He would legislate.

For several years Roosevelt's brain trust had been anticipating this assault on the Constitution's separation of powers. Two of the most important framers of the New Deal, James Landis and Felix Frankfurter, called the doctrine that Congress cannot delegate its legislative powers to an executive agency a "jejune abstraction."[11] According to Landis, the doctrine "retired from the field" because of "the inadequacy of a simply tripartite form of government to deal with modern problems." So long as Congress specifies "the end which regulation seeks to attain"—such as establishing fair prices, fighting fraud, or protecting public safety—it does not matter if "the standards as written into the legislation are broad and vague."[12]

With Landis's help, the Roosevelt administration persuaded Congress to delegate away its power, creating a host of agencies that would make rules to govern the American people. Congress created the Securities and Exchange Commission; Federal Communications Commission; Social Security Administration; Farm Credit Administration; Farm Security Administration; Federal Deposit Insurance Corporation; Federal Savings and Loan Insurance Corporation; Federal National Mortgage Association; U.S. Housing Authority; Federal Housing Administration; and Civil Aeronautics Board. With an executive order, the president also created the National Labor Relations Board.[13] Each of these bureaucracies would both create and enforce regulations.

Several of these agencies were designed to meet important needs. But in keeping with the Roosevelt-Landis vision of an executive branch that can legislate, the statutes that created these agencies often gave them almost unlimited discretion in making rules related to their subject matter. The Federal Communications Commission could regulate in any way that "public interest, convenience, or necessity requires."[14] The Office of Price Administration could set commodity prices at any level, so long as they were "fair and equitable."[15] Under a title in the Agricultural Marketing Agreement Act, the secretary of agriculture could issue marketing orders placing limits on the sale of certain farm products when the limits "will tend to effectuate the declared policy of this title."[16] Rather than Congress deciding which rules might be in the "public interest" or "fair and equitable" or necessary "to effectuate the declared policy," the president and his executive agencies would now decide—just as a monarch might.

"People Came for Miles to Take the Fruit, But This Could Not Be"

The transfer of legislative power from Congress to the president's agencies was—and remains—a profound threat to representative government, as shown by Congress's seemingly benign decision during the Dust Bowl to authorize the Department of Agriculture to put quotas on the sale of agricultural commodities. Congress's motive was to help farmers by boosting the prices of goods like milk, almonds, and oranges. But like most benefits to one group, this aid to farmers came at a cost to other groups. The quotas chosen by the Agriculture Department hurt hardworking American consumers by inflating the price of food. They also ensured that, at a time when many people were starving, enormous quantities of food were kept from the marketplace.

In *The Grapes of Wrath* John Steinbeck describes "carloads of oranges dumped on the ground." In his story, "people came for miles to take the fruit, but this could not be." Powerful interests wanted these hungry people to "buy oranges at twenty cents a dozen," and that wouldn't happen if "they could drive out and pick them up." To keep the starving citizens away from the rotting oranges, "men with hoses squirt kerosene on the oranges, and they are angry at the crime, angry at the people who have come to take the fruit."[17]

Although Steinbeck's *The Grapes of Wrath* is fictional, the scene is based on actual policies. As Professor David Schoenbrod has described, from 1933 to 1992 agricultural marketing orders prevented one third of navel oranges from being sold in the American fresh-fruit market. Although some of those oranges were exported, most were turned into juice or cattle feed—or allowed to rot.[18]

In the normal course, bad policies that hurt the citizenry can be repealed by the people's representatives. Not so with the quotas on oranges. The people's elected officials in Congress were no longer in charge of the policy. The agency officials set the policies, and the people were powerless.

Before long, the policy of putting quotas on oranges went from bad to worse. A Navel Orange Administrative Committee created by the Department of Agriculture began setting the policy, and Sunkist, a titan in the orange industry, was given outsized influence over the committee. It could nominate five of the eleven commissioners. A direct phone line connected Sunkist and the committee. The committee's staff even earned coverage under Sunkist's pension plan.[19] This was crony capitalism at its worst, all facilitated by a dangerous deviation from our constitutional structure.

The story of overpriced oranges may seem mundane, but agricultural marketing orders increased the grocery bills of American families by hundreds of dollars every year.[20] Many orange farmers were suffering from the quotas as well because Sunkist was able to make the marketing orders correspond with its own plans while imposing extra costs on small farmers.[21]

If constituents paying inflated grocery bills complained to their members of Congress—including members receiving campaign contributions from Sunkist—the legislators could blame the quotas on the Department of Agriculture. Some congressmen even wrote letters to the secretary of agriculture urging an end to the quotas in order to help feed starving children—as if letter writing, rather than legislating, were the job of legislators.[22] But when laws are made by monarchs, or by unelected officials unaccountable to the people, what else is there to do?

Marching in Protest Against a Law They Supported

Since the advent of delegation to executive agencies, this cycle has repeated itself hundreds—perhaps thousands—of times. Congressmen claim credit for passing a statute with lofty promises, such as stabilizing the market for farmers. Then, in the face of their constituents' criticism of an agency-made policy that harms them by fulfilling those promises, congressmen criticize the policy without having to actually vote against it.

Consider the costs of reducing air pollution. The Environmental Protection Agency's clean-air regulations cost Americans tens of billions of dollars every year.[23] They result in higher electric bills; fewer jobs and lower wages for coal miners, car makers, and other workers; and less value for anyone who has invested (either directly or through a mutual fund or retirement plan) in a company that produces or uses energy—in other words, almost any company in America.[24]

For good reason, we as a society have decided that this price (that is, the price of clean air) should be paid. But in imposing these billions of dollars of costs, there are countless difficult decisions to be made—decisions that inevitably involve a balancing of the costs and benefits of each possible restriction and culminate in a determination as to which costs are worth bearing and who will bear them. New power plants or old power plants? Car owners or electricity users? States that rely on coal or states that rely on natural gas?

While promising to reduce air pollution, the Clean Air Act answered almost none of these hard questions. It simply told the EPA to put whatever limits on pollutants the agency deemed "requisite to protect the public health" with an "adequate margin for safety." Hardly anyone was against this law—until they became the ones who had to pay for it.

Among the most enthusiastic advocates for the law were New York's liberal congressmen and their constituents. Opposing the bill before its passage would have been outright heresy at an Upper West Side cocktail party. But several years later, when the Clean Air Act was used to impose tolls on New York City's bridges in order to increase funds for public transportation, city dwellers balked.

Sure, people in New York City wanted less pollution. Sure, improving mass transit would reduce automotive pollution. But tolls on bridges? That was going to hit New Yorkers right in their pocketbooks. After all, they lived on and around an island; how dare anyone charge them money to cross a bridge!

Of course, the tolls were the result of the law that New York City's congressmen had championed. If liberal legislators had voted *against* the Clean Air Act, they might well have been voted out of office for opposing it. But by declining to make hard choices in the act, Congress had empowered *others* to make those choices. And when those choices were made in a way that hurt those legislators' constituents, the congressmen feigned outrage. They even marched in protest across the Brooklyn Bridge. Only in the bizarre world of delegating legislative powers could members of Congress lead a march in protest against the consequences of a law they voted for.

How Courts Have Abdicated Their Responsibility

Because executive agencies aren't accountable to the public, they often make rules that no elected official could ever defend with a straight face—like the rules made possible by the Clean Water Act.

Like the Clean Air Act, the Clean Water Act was relatively easy for legislators to vote for. Its stated goal was "to restore and maintain the chemical, physical, and biological integrity of the Nation's water," while delegating the difficult and costly details to executive agencies. The statute was all gain, with no pain—at least on its face. But it wasn't long before Congress's delegation of the hard choices it refused to make created a kind of Frankenstein's monster—all powerful, at times nonsensical, and impossible to control.

The Clean Water Act requires landowners to obtain a permit before they discharge materials into "the waters of the United States." But what does that mean? Everyone would agree that the Mississippi River is among "the waters of the United States." The same goes for the American portions of Lake Michigan and the Gulf of Mexico. But what about small ponds? Babbling brooks? Swamps? Marshes? Bogs? Puddles that don't dry quickly?

Empowered by Congress to create its own definition of "waters of the United States," the EPA and Army Corps of Engineers have decided that those "waters" include pretty much all of the above. In their words, "waters" include "areas that are inundated or saturated by surface or ground water at a frequency and duration sufficient to support, and that under normal circumstances do support, a prevalence of vegetation typically adapted for life in saturated soil conditions."[25] In plain English, that means that "waters of the United States" can include just about "any piece of land that is wet at least part of the year."[26] If your backyard is soggy for one week out of fifty-two, there's a chance the EPA can prevent you from building anything on it larger than a doghouse.[27]

Ocie Mills and his son Carey learned about the dangers of legislative delegation the hard way. They bought a wooded plot of land with a skinny stretch of marsh grass on it.[28] The land overlooked Florida's Escambia Bay, and the father and son decided to build a house on part of it.

After building began, the U.S. government prosecuted them for violating the Clean Water Act. A jury in Florida found them guilty, and both were later sentenced to two years and nine months in prison.

The Millses had committed the crime of discharging a "pollutant" into "the navigable waters of the United States." In their case, the "pollutant" was dry sand used for building a house, and the "water" was a piece of dry, wooded land that met the agencies' definition of "navigable waters" because of its small strip of marsh grass, which was not even on the part of the property where the house was being built.[29]

The judge assigned to the case, Roger Vinson, sympathized with the Millses. He admitted that a "layman" would not expect "waters" to include "land that appears to be dry, but which may have some saturated-soil vegetation, as is the situation here." But his hands were tied by an agency rule that was the product of Congress's decision "to abdicate its power to define the elements of a criminal offense."

The law that ensnared Ocie and Carey Mills is far from unique. Some experts estimate that the number of criminally enforceable federal regulations exceeds 300,000.[30] In a three-year span, federal prosecutors obtained sentences of around three hundred years of prison time and millions of dollars in fines in four hundred cases that all arose from environmental regulations.[31] Congress even authorized an entirely new agency to decide the sentencing ranges applicable to criminal violations of federal regulations; having already delegated to various agencies the task of *making* the criminal laws at issue, Congress delegated to yet another agency the task of determining how anyone violating those laws would be punished![32]

For a brief time in the 1920s and 1930s, the Supreme Court tried to police this kind of delegation. But after an attack on the Court by a popular and powerful president—Franklin Roosevelt—the Court quickly gave up protecting the Constitution in order to protect itself. As Judge Vinson explained, that surrender "does violence to [the] time-honored principle" that the "definition of the elements of a criminal offense is entrusted to the legislature." When Congress "abdicate[s] its power to define the elements of a criminal offense, in favor of an un-elected administrative agency," the delegation "calls into question the vitality of the tripartite system established by our Constitution."[33]

Several members of the current Supreme Court have echoed Judge Vinson's concern in one way or another. They probably find it as absurd as you do that, for example, a single statute empowering the Food and Drug Administration to make rules for "medical devices" has led to the FDA's regulation of weight-lifting equipment, mouthwash, sunglasses, and television remote controls.[34] At least some of them appear to agree that the legislative branch is supposed to make laws, not lawmakers. But a majority of the Court insists that it lacks the institutional capacity to combat Congress's excessive delegation of lawmaking power. According to this view, it is too hard to draw sufficiently clear legal lines between permissible agency action and unconstitutional delegation, so only the people can control Congress on this matter, using the power they wield at the ballot box to require their representatives to follow the Constitution and stand accountable for federal laws made on their watch.

A Hidden Tax on Every American

Even if, unlike Ocie and Carey Mills, we never find ourselves in the prosecutorial crosshairs of federal regulators, the rules they impose on this nation affect our lives in a profound way by imposing a jaw-droppingly large and hidden tax on each and every one of us.

I was stunned to learn just how expensive those rules are when I was in law school. Our chapter of the Federalist Society hosted a speech by Lawrence Block (now a judge on the U.S. Court of Federal Claims), who was then senior counsel to the Senate Judiciary

Committee. In the middle of his talk, Block explained that federal regulations impose an invisible, backdoor tax on the American people, because the cost of complying with the regulations is passed on to consumers and workers in the form of higher prices. Products ranging from navel oranges to automobiles become more expensive to produce as a result of federal regulations, so manufacturers charge their customers more. Compliance also causes lower wages and unemployment, since employers have less money to devote to payroll as the cost of doing business increases due to federal regulations.

So far, Block had not said anything that I found surprising, but that changed when he stated the annual cost of compliance with federal regulations. It was around $300 billion! There was an audible gasp in the room. We were young, conservative law students who considered ourselves skeptics of a large federal government, but few of us had imagined that the cost of regulations written by unaccountable federal bureaucrats was anywhere near $300 billion.

I remember to this day how outraged I was. *If this is true,* I said to myself, *it's got to be stopped.* But rather than being stopped, it has multiplied. The hidden tax imposed by agency regulations is now roughly *$2 trillion* per year. That's $6,666 for every man, woman, and child in America—more than $33,000 for my family of five.

This $2 trillion "tax" is far more dangerous than traditional taxes, because the American people have little recourse for reducing its burden or even opposing its growth. If constituents complain about the cost of a regulation to a member of Congress, he can reply, "Well, I didn't vote for that particular regulation. I voted for clean air [or clean water or safe medical devices or fair farming markets]. If you don't like how that law was applied by the EPA [or the Army Corps of Engineers or the FDA or the Department of Agriculture], your complaint is with them, not me." If the congressman is feeling energetic, he might offer to write the agency a letter about starving children—or lead a protest march across the Brooklyn Bridge—

even though the agency is not accountable (at least not directly) to Congress or the people Congress represents.

"If Congress Won't Act . . . I Will"

It has been eight decades since President Franklin Roosevelt called for a "temporary departure from that normal balance" between "executive and legislative authority." The crisis he treated like "the emergency of a war" has long passed, but the "normal balance" never returned. Instead, the unaccountable administrative state is bigger than ever. To Roosevelt's agencies have been added relatively well-known agencies like the Equal Employment Opportunity Commission and the Occupational Safety and Health Administration. The administrative state also includes more than *three hundred* other agencies, from the Office of English Language Acquisition to the Committee for Purchase from People Who Are Blind or Severely Disabled.[35]

This state of affairs is nothing like the system of representative government found by Alexis de Tocqueville on his visit to the United States in 1835. The Frenchman was able to report to his countrymen that in the United States "the nation participates in the making of its laws by the choice of its legislators, and in the execution of them by the choice of agents of the executive government." No visitor to the United States could truthfully write those words today. Nor could that visitor conclude, as Tocqueville did, that "so feeble and so restricted is the share left to the administrators, so little do the authorities forget their popular origins and the power from which they emanate."[36]

A return to the system the founders created and Tocqueville described would enhance the liberty of all Americans, regardless of their political persuasions. It would return control over the federal government to Republican and Democratic citizens alike, which explains why today's administrative Leviathan has faced criticism not only from Republicans like me but from former Democratic senator Bill Bradley, by the American Civil Liberties Union, and in the pages of the *New Republic*. Writing for that magazine, Jacob Weisberg lamented the fact that the federal government can "now penetrate every nook and cranny of American life in a way that was simply impossible before" the delegation of legislative power. This delegation has functioned as "a labor-saving device" that "did for legislators what the washing machine did for the 1950s housewife."[37]

Nevertheless, although a few liberals have criticized the unaccountable nature of the administrative state, many more of them have welcomed it as a mechanism for policing American industry and enterprise when the people's representatives in Congress are unwilling to grant the Far Left's wish list of regulations.

One recent example of a president bypassing Congress is President Obama's attempt to control the climate through an aggressive reading of the Clean Air Act. In his first term, the president tried and failed to persuade a *Democratic* Congress to enact a cap-and-trade bill. The proposal threatened to cost 2.5 million jobs and siphon off more than $9 trillion from the U.S. economy over twenty-five years.[38] When a bipartisan coalition in Congress stopped the bill dead in its tracks, the president decided to blatantly disregard the will of the people, reject the separation of powers crafted by our founders, and use the Environmental Protection Agency to impose on Americans the laws that their elected representatives refused to make. "If Congress won't act," he declared, "I will."

Of course, I can understand why Barack Obama wants to see his preferred policies become law. It can be frustrating when the checks and balances of our system block a policy that one believes is in the nation's best interest. But the Constitution separates the federal government's powers for a simple purpose: to preserve liberty. As the Supreme Court explained in a case my father argued and won, "the choices we discern as having been made in the Constitutional Convention impose burdens on governmental processes that often seem clumsy, inefficient, even unworkable, but those hard choices were consciously made by men who had lived under a form of government that permitted arbitrary governmental acts to go unchecked."[39]

When Congress delegates its legislative powers to federal bureaucrats unelected and unaccountable to the American people, it creates a government in which "arbitrary governmental acts . . . go unchecked." It ignores the first line of the first article of the Constitution: "All legislative Powers herein granted shall be vested in a Congress of the United States." It makes real a world not entirely unlike that imagined by the brilliant but misguided Alexander Hamilton, who envisioned an elected monarch for his country. And it subjects us to the kind of executive—roundly rejected by Hamilton's fellow delegates in Philadelphia—who can say, "If Congress won't act . . . I will."

Those are not the words of a president.

Those are the words of a king.

CHAPTER 4

The Supreme Court's Klansman

THE FORGOTTEN ESTABLISHMENT CLAUSE

Congress shall make no law respecting an establishment of religion.

—UNITED STATES CONSTITUTION, FIRST AMENDMENT

FOR MORE THAN A CENTURY AND A HALF AFTER THE FOUNDING of our nation, the First Amendment was not interpreted as requiring the government to be completely neutral between religion and atheism. National leaders repeatedly called the nation to prayer, lent modest support to religious institutions, and mixed religion with government. The First Congress encouraged religious schools by granting them federal land in the Northwest Territory.[1] Congressional sessions and federal court proceedings across the country began with a prayer. Currency said "In God We Trust."[2] Federal officials prominently displayed the Ten Commandments. The capitol building even hosted church services. Presidents Washington, Adams, and Madison issued Thanksgiving proclamations calling for prayer and fasting because it was "the duty of all nations to acknowledge the providence of Almighty God, to obey His will, to be grateful for His benefits, and humbly to implore His protection and favor."[3]

President Thomas Jefferson—no enemy of religious freedom—signed a treaty with the Kaskaskia Indians that provided federal funds to support their Catholic priest and church. Those funds eventually totaled $500,000 per year.[4]

Since 1947, federal courts have led this nation on a dramatic and distressing detour from this tradition. For example, in 2010 a federal court found it unconstitutional when the state of Utah displayed white crosses on public lands to honor highway patrolmen who died there in the line of duty. The judges arrived at that decision even though not a single family of the fallen objected to the memorials (and even though the Church of Jesus Christ of Latter-day Saints, whose members are a majority in Utah, does not use the cross as a symbol of its faith). In a series of other confusing and often conflicting cases, courts have at times required the Ten Commandments to be removed from a courthouse,[5] a Christmas crèche to be kept off a county courthouse's steps,[6] and a city seal to exclude religious symbols.[7]

Courts have also taken aim at public and parochial schools. They have declared it unconstitutional for a public-school teacher to lead students in a voluntary prayer,[8] for public-school students to be afforded a moment of silence "for meditation or voluntary prayer,"[9] and even for a public-school student to pray out loud over his lunch.[10] With regard to parochial schools, it was found unconstitutional when a state funded counseling inside the school,[11] speech and hearing services in the school building,[12] or busing for a field trip to the zoo.[13] It has also been held unconstitutional for a state or local government to lend a parochial school maps for a geography class,[14] a film projector for a history class,[15] or even a movie about George Washington.[16]

So how did we get from our first president proclaiming obedience to God's will the duty of the nation to forbidding a child from praying over his school lunch? The answer lies in the story of how judges and legislators have misinterpreted the First Amendment's establishment clause.

The establishment clause provides that "Congress shall make no law respecting an establishment of religion." In recent decades, courts and legislators have forgotten the clause's true meaning in two ways.

Their first mistake is their belief that a government "establishes" a religion when it uses a cross to honor fallen policemen, allows students a moment of silence at the beginning of the school day, or lends a film about the father of our country to a Catholic school. That is nonsense. Government "establishes" a religion only when it declares a particular denomination to be the religion of the state, props up the religious exercises of a particular denomination with public funds, or coerces individuals into participating in the rituals of a particular denomination.

Their second mistake is what made the first mistake possible, and it is the topic of this chapter. Contrary to the views of most judges and legislators, the establishment clause applies *only* to the federal government. It does not put any limits on state governments. In fact, the establishment clause's purpose is to *allow* states, cities, and local school boards to make their own choices about the role of religion in the public arena, free from federal interference.

As Supreme Court justice Potter Stewart wrote in 1963, "it is not without irony that a constitutional provision evidently designed to leave the States free to go their own way should now have become a restriction upon their autonomy."

This chapter tells the story of how that irony became a reality. It begins by showing the role of religion in the founding era and the purpose, as well as the limits, of the establishment clause. Then it follows the rise of a Ku Klux Klansman from the courtrooms of Alabama to his seat on the Supreme Court of the United States, where, in 1947, he led the Court in erroneously applying the establishment clause to state and local governments.

In telling this story, it is important to make clear what my purpose is—and what it is not. Needless to say, I do not believe any state should establish a religion. Even though the establishment clause does not preclude states from doing so, I would never want to live in a state that made that choice, which our modern society rightly regards as foolish and intolerant.

My only purpose in this chapter is to show how the decision to apply the establishment clause to state governments was made, why it was wrong, and how it has made possible all the mischief that the majority of Americans *do* oppose—such as prohibitions on voluntary prayer in schools and bans on nativity scenes at Christmastime. Once we understand that history, we can demand that our legislators and judges resurrect the true meaning of the lost establishment clause—which puts no limits on state governments. Only then will the people of each state once again be free to decide for themselves whether to put a memorial in the form of a cross on a highway and whether to help fund the secular education of children whose parents choose parochial schools.

I have no doubt that if given the choice the First Amendment offers them, no states would establish a religion. That is certainly a good thing. But I also have no doubt that if given the choice, many communities would choose to enjoy more opportunities for public worship and religious reflection than federal courts have allowed them. That, too, would be a good thing, because as Justice Antonin Scalia has explained, religion is not "some purely personal avocation that can be indulged entirely in secret, like pornography, in the privacy of one's room."[17]

Instead, throughout our history, "men and women of almost all denominations have felt it necessary to acknowledge and beseech the blessing of God as a people, and not just as individuals, because they believe in the 'protection of divine Providence,' as the Declaration of Independence put it, not just for individuals but for societies; because they believe God to be, as Washington's first Thanksgiving Proclamation put it, the 'Great Lord and Ruler of Nations.'"[18]

There was once a time when "We the People" were able to do exactly that.

We should be able to do so again.

"Public Protestant Teachers of Piety"

In the office off the front hall of his small farmhouse, the stocky lawyer stood before his tall desk, pen in hand, intensely reading and rereading the words of Charles de Montesquieu, John Locke, and the Virginia Declaration of Rights. The newly independent Commonwealth of Massachusetts needed a constitution, and the delegates to its constitutional convention had chosen John Adams to write it. This was a weighty responsibility, and Adams was looking to the great minds of history for help.

Three years earlier, in 1776, Adams had represented Massachusetts at the Continental Congress. He had been among its most ferocious advocates for independence. But like most of his fellow revolutionaries, Adams had not merely opposed *his* monarch. He had been against *all* monarchs. And now, alone in his office with only the well-worn pages of his books to assist him, he embarked on the task of turning the blank paper before him into a framework for an alternative to monarchy—into a republican commonwealth.

Certain elements of the new political system were taken for granted in Adams's Massachusetts. There would be a "social compact" between the government and the governed. Citizens would choose their representatives. Those representatives would respect and protect the natural rights of those citizens. "The end of the institution, maintenance and administration of government," wrote

Adams in the first sentence of the Massachusetts Constitution's pre-amble, "is to secure the existence of the body-politic; to protect it; and to furnish the individuals who compose it, with the power of enjoying, in safety and tranquility, their natural rights, and the blessings of life."

The question, however, was how to structure a government to ac-complish that "end." For John Adams, the answer was to begin with a declaration of rights.

As written by Adams, slightly amended by the convention, and ratified by the people of his state, the Massachusetts Constitution's Declaration of Rights provides for a bicameral legislature filled by "free" and "regular elections." It protects "life, liberty and property." It guarantees the "liberty of the press" and the "right to keep and to bear arms." It prohibits "unreasonable searches and seizures." It cre-ates a "free, impartial and independent" judiciary. And it establishes extensive safeguards for the criminally accused, with provisions for "trial by jury," confrontation of witnesses "face to face," and the right of a defendant not to "furnish evidence against himself."

In the declaration's most memorable article, Adams enshrined the principle of separation of powers with an eloquence that would be remembered and repeated for ages—often without attribution. "In the government of this Commonwealth," wrote Adams, "the legislative department shall never exercise the executive and judicial powers, or either of them: The executive shall never exercise the leg-islative and judicial powers, or either of them: The judicial shall never exercise the legislative and executive powers, or either of them: *to the end it may be a government of laws and not of men.*"

If that line is the Massachusetts Constitution's Declaration of Rights's most famous, its most forgotten provision is a lengthy blue-print for the establishment of religion. The declaration called "wor-ship" of "the Supreme Being" not only a right but also "the duty of all men." It stated that "the happiness of a people, and the good order and preservation of civil government, essentially depend upon piety, religion and morality." According to the declaration, "these cannot be generally diffused through a community, but by the institution of the public worship of God, and of public instructions in piety, religion and morality."

To provide for public provisions for worship, the third article of the Massachusetts Constitution's Declaration of Rights allowed towns to tax residents to fund a town-sponsored church. It provided that towns might "make suitable provision, at their own expense, for the institution of the public worship of God, and for the support and maintenance of public protestant teachers of piety, religion and morality." A member of a religious minority could direct that his taxes fund "his own religious sect or denomination, provided there be any on whose instructions he attends," but if he did not attend a church, his taxes would "be paid toward the support of the teacher or teachers of the parish or precinct."

In addition, the Massachusetts Constitution's Declaration of Rights allowed towns to make it a crime to skip church services. The legislature could "enjoin upon all the subjects an attendance upon the instructions of the public teachers aforesaid, at stated times and seasons, if there be any on whose instructions they can conscientiously and conveniently attend." Over the next several decades, grand juries in the state issued more indictments for failing to attend church than for any other crime.

By establishing government-sponsored religion in Massachusetts, Adams's constitution was following in a long tradition with which Americans of the era were quite familiar. Christopher Columbus considered his discovery of the New World in 1492 to be an "enterprise in the name of our Savior."[19] Great Britain's first colonial grant in 1584 authorized Sir Walter Raleigh to make laws "not against the true Christian faith."[20] Virginia's first charter in 1606 provided for "propagating of Christian Religion."[21] The Mayflower Compact of

1620 included among its purposes the "advancement of the Christian faith."[22] The charters and founding-era documents of the Massachusetts, Maryland, North Carolina, Rhode Island, Pennsylvania, Connecticut, New Hampshire, and New Jersey colonies differed in the extent of religious freedom they provided to Christian colonists of differing denominations, but they all referred to the "Christian faith" or the "Christian religion" as a foundation of the colonial project.

In light of this history, it is easy to see why John Adams included the establishment of religion in the Massachusetts Constitution. Adams, the attorney for British soldiers prosecuted for the Boston Massacre, was among the great civil libertarians of his time. But even Adams considered the establishment of religion to be entirely consistent with democratic principles like free elections, checks and balances, the right to speak freely, and the free exercise of religion. In fact, so ingrained in society was government-sponsored religion that it is doubtful the people of Massachusetts would have ratified a constitution that did not provide for towns' establishments of religious faiths.

In this the people of Massachusetts were not alone. By the end of the 1780s, churches in six states—Massachusetts, New Hampshire, Connecticut, Maryland, South Carolina, and Georgia—were supported by the government.[23] When Vermont became a state in 1791, it brought this number up to seven.[24] Two states—Delaware and Maryland—required legislators to profess their faith in Christianity. Five states—New Hampshire, Massachusetts, Connecticut, Maryland, and South Carolina—demanded Protestantism. Four states—Pennsylvania, Delaware, North Carolina, and South Carolina—limited seats in the legislature to citizens who believed that the Bible was the word of God.[25]

Today we know better. We see the concept of a state-sponsored religion as unjust. We realize that our nation's religious diversity is a source of strength. We would be appalled at any kind of religious test for public office. We—particularly those of us who, like me, are members of a religious minority—would never wish to return to an era in which states and localities declared one faith to be *the* faith.

But in order to understand the meaning and limits of our nation's First Amendment, we must understand the era that produced it. We must remember that it was a time when, although Americans were generally free to exercise their own religious practices, state-sponsored religion was the norm throughout much of the nation—so much so that even the civil libertarian John Adams enshrined it in the Massachusetts Constitution. And we must look closely at what the founding generation wanted to preserve when they ratified the First Amendment and the Bill of Rights.

The Establishment Clause Is Born

Nearly ten years after John Adams began writing the Massachusetts Constitution, James Madison rose to his feet in the House of Representatives in August of 1789 to propose what he had spent nearly a year calling unnecessary—a bill of rights for the United States Constitution.

"It appears to me that this House is bound by every motive of prudence," Madison declared from the House floor, "not to let the first session pass over without proposing to the State Legislatures, some things to be incorporated into the Constitution, that will render it as acceptable to the whole people of the United States, as it has been found acceptable to a majority of them."[26]

Much had changed since Adams had written his state's constitution, and Madison's words reflected those changes. In the past ten years, the United States had won its independence, faltered under the Articles of Confederation, and replaced them with the Constitution that Madison had made possible in Philadelphia. But Madison's struggle for the Constitution had not ended upon its drafting in the City of Brotherly Love. It could not become law until conventions in nine states ratified it, and the fight for ratification that began in 1787 had proven long and arduous. Steadfast and powerful blocs in most states believed that the newly proposed government was too big, too distant, and far too powerful. Resistance to it was so intense that opponents burned copies of it at a July 4 parade in New York, where violence erupted. Eighteen people were wounded. One died.

Dubbed by the Federalist supporters of the Constitution as the Anti-Federalists, opponents of the new Constitution had been alarmed by the federal Constitution's omission of a bill of rights. They included in their ranks Revolutionary War heroes like Patrick Henry and Samuel Adams, who were not persuaded by Madison's argument in 1787 that there was no point in a bill of rights listing things the national government could *not* do, when it was already clear the national government could do *nothing* other than what was listed in the Constitution.

The Anti-Federalists presciently saw that ambiguities in the Constitution would lead to a gradual expansion of federal power. They believed that over time, without a bill of rights, majority factions in the country would use the federal government's powers to violate property rights, persecute political opponents, or impose a national religion on states that had established a different religion. So powerful were their arguments that a switch of 10 votes (out of 355 cast) would have defeated the Constitution at the ratifying convention in Massachusetts, and a switch of just 2 votes (out of 57) would have doomed it at New York's.

By 1789, having narrowly defeated the Anti-Federalists, Madison was able to rise in Congress and say that the Constitution had "been found acceptable to a majority" of the American people. But the Anti-Federalists' defeat was not unconditional. Toward the end of the struggle for ratification, Madison and his allies had agreed to a bill of rights in exchange for ratification. For a few of the Constitution's skeptics—just enough of them—this promise had been sufficient to make ratification possible.

By keeping his promise, Madison hoped to render the Constitution "acceptable to the whole people." And in proposing a bill of rights, Madison was not without guidance about what would render it "acceptable." Countless Anti-Federalist writers and politicians had proposed amendments. Five of the eleven states that had ratified the Constitution had proposed specific amendments. The remaining two were refusing to ratify until similar amendments were added. It was Madison's job to write a bill of rights that incorporated the most important and popular of the proposed amendments.

Most of these proposals for a bill of rights included a prohibition against the establishment of a national religion. The concern was clear: No one wanted the new federal government to get in the way of each state having the power to establish its own religion. Thus, when Madison proposed amendments to be included in the Bill of Rights, he proposed a guarantee that no "national religion" shall "be established." After congressional debate and a conference committee to combine a similar amendment passed by the Senate, the Bill of Rights read, "Congress shall make no law respecting an establishment of religion, or prohibiting the free exercise thereof." When it was ratified by the states, it became the first guarantee of the First Amendment.

Like the Tenth Amendment, which "reserved to the States" the "powers not delegated to the United States," the establishment clause reserved to the states the power to establish—or disestablish—a religion, by forbidding the federal government from interfering with each state's prerogative. As Supreme Court Justice Joseph Story, one of his generation's most respected legal analysts, wrote in 1833, "The real object of the First Amendment was . . . to prevent any national ecclesiastical establishment" by leaving "the whole power over the subject of religion . . . exclusively to the state governments."[27]

This view of the establishment clause explains why six states continued to establish a religion *after* the First Amendment was ratified and why Massachusetts did not end its establishment of religion until 1833 (becoming the last state to do so). It makes clear how it was possible for states like Massachusetts—governed by constitutions like that written by John Adams—to prosecute citizens for not attending church services decades after the First Amendment was ratified. It explains why not one of the states with constitutions that established religions objected to the First Amendment.

In the past sixty-eight years, however, many judges and legislators have acted as if the establishment clause protects people from state governments' laws on religion, rather than protecting state governments from the federal government's interference with their laws on religion.

The story of how the establishment clause's true meaning was lost begins at a murder trial in Birmingham, Alabama.

The trial was part of a battle against the Catholic Church.

The battle was waged by the Ku Klux Klan.

"Your Girl Is a Catholic and She Is Married, for I Married Her This Evening"

The Reverend Edwin Stephenson stood in the rectory of Saint Paul's Catholic Church, his pistol in his pocket, staring with anger at Father James Coyle. Earlier on this late-summer day in 1921, his eighteen-year-old daughter Ruth had gone missing, and Stephenson was sure Father Coyle had something to do with her disappearance.[28]

Stephenson was an abusive father. Last winter he had whipped Ruth for staying out past nine thirty at night. On another occasion he had locked his daughter in her room for three days without food or water. Not that his rage was aimed only at his own family. Stephenson had joined in the lynching of an African American in 1902.

A decade and a half later he had shot a barber in his hometown of Birmingham.

If Father Coyle had known of Stephenson's penchant for violence, he might have chosen his words more carefully. But because Coyle didn't, he told the stranger with the handlebar mustache exactly where Ruth was—with her husband.

"Well, my girl isn't married," snarled Stephenson.

"Your girl is a Catholic and she is married," said Coyle calmly, "for I married her this evening."

"To whom?" asked a stunned Stephenson.

"To Pedro Gussman," said Coyle, "a Catholic."

There was not any news that would have enraged Stephenson more than the words he heard. He had once said he wished the "whole Catholic institution was in hell." But now his daughter was married to a Catholic. And to a Puerto Rican one at that! Gussman had once hung wallpaper at the Stephensons' home.

"You have married her to that n*****!" shouted Stephenson. "You have treated me dirtier than a dog! You have acted like a dirty, low-down, yellow dog!"

Moments later, several shots rang out.

An unarmed Father James Coyle lay dead on the floor of his home.

Before long, the Ku Klux Klan had arranged a dream team of lawyers for Edwin Stephenson. At the head of that team was Hugo Lafayette Black.

"Bring Him Closer to the Jury, and Let Them See His Eyes"

A high-school dropout who had taken up the law after failing the state teachers' exam, the thirty-five-year-old Hugo Black was, by 1921, among Birmingham's best attorneys. With his country accent and likable manner, the former farm boy with the long nose, thin frame, and sparkling eyes was the quintessential southern lawyer—well connected, comfortable on his feet, and a natural at playing on the emotions of a jury.

In the trial of Edwin Stephenson for second-degree murder, Black knew exactly where his jury's emotions were likely to lie. They were not about to sympathize with a dead Catholic priest who had, as Black told the jurors, "proselytized" a "child of a Methodist" and "planted in her mind the seeds of influence" that caused her to "depart from her religion."

Nor were they likely to believe the Catholic witnesses called by the prosecution. "You are a Catholic, aren't you?" Black asked each of them. When they admitted they were, Black dismissed them with a two-word reply: "That's all." Later, he called the Catholic witnesses "Siamese twins" who were "brothers of falsehood as well as faith."

By the early 1920s, anti-Catholic prejudice was at its height, and at the vanguard of that bigotry was the Ku Klux Klan. After decades of dormancy, the secret organization had been reorganized in 1915 amid rising hostility toward the millions of Catholic and Jewish immigrants arriving at ports like Ellis Island. The Klan's imperial wizard called the Catholic Church "actually and actively alien, un-American and usually anti-American." The United States "must remain Protestant, if the Nordic stock is to finish its destiny."[29] Under this banner of intolerance, the Klan's membership swelled to five million white-robed terrorists and vigilantes.

In Birmingham the Ku Klux Klan controlled the police, the courts, and the local government. Its members marched in parades carrying shotguns and "peering like white, pointy-headed owls from under their sheets, with only their shoes visible."[30] Among the routine elements of life in the early 1920s were burning crosses, kidnappings, brutal beatings and floggings, brandings with hot irons, and tar and featherings.

Few if any of the men behind these crimes were ever convicted. Juries were dominated by Klansmen, who systematically acquitted any white Protestant accused of beating, torturing, shooting, or lynching an African American, a Catholic, or an immigrant.

It was in this state of Klan domination that Hugo Black defended Edwin Stephenson. Although not yet a Klansman himself, Black knew his audience. A majority of the jurors wore the white robes of the Klan, as did their foreman, who was a field organizer. So did the judge.

Black understood that these men were inclined to share his client's intolerance not only toward religious minorities but toward ethnic minorities as well. They were sure to be outraged not only by Father Coyle's supposed brainwashing of a good Protestant girl but also by his act of marrying her to a Hispanic groom. When Black questioned Stephenson on the witness stand, his client told him, "You can call him a Puerto Rican, but to me he's a n*****."

A talented and shameless showman, Black ended his direct examination of Stephenson with a stunt straight out of Hollywood. He had the blinds of the courtroom closed. He had the lights dimmed. Then he told the bailiff, "Call Pedro Gussman in."

As Edwin Stephenson's wife fought back tears with a handkerchief, Black asked Stephenson, "Is this the Pedro Gussman you referred to?"

"Yes," said Stephenson.

"Bring him closer to the jury," said Black, "and let them see his eyes."

Suddenly, as Gussman was standing in silence before the jury box, floodlights installed by Black switched on and shot beams of light in the darkened room at the stunned and confused Gussman.

The jurors looked upon him with disgust, just as Black knew they would. He wanted them to hate Gussman for sharing the bed of a white woman Black repeatedly referred to as a "girl." He wanted them to blame Gussman for tearing apart a good southern family. And he wanted them to look at Gussman's dark skin and slicked-back black hair and believe that Edwin Stephenson had had no choice but to avenge his family's honor.

"That will do," said Black after what surely seemed to Gussman like a lifetime. "I just wanted the jury to see that man."

Days later, Black was even more explicit in his appeal to the jury's southern "honor," especially with regard to those jurors who had sworn secret oaths to defend white supremacy. "Our Father and our God," he said, "harmonize our souls with the sacred principles and purposes of our noble Order that we may keep our sacred oath inviolate."

Those were the words of the official prayer of the Ku Klux Klan.

Black then attacked the credibility of Catholic witnesses, told the jury that Puerto Rico was full of "mulattoes," and painted a vivid picture of the Stephensons returning to a house made empty by a daughter lost to Pedro Gussman and the Roman Catholic Church. "If the eyes of the world are upon the verdict of this jury," declared Black, "I would write that verdict in words that cannot be misunderstood, that the homes of the people of Birmingham cannot be touched. If that brings disgrace, God hasten the disgrace."

Few eyes in the courtroom were dry.

The prosecutors' closing arguments that followed were futile.

Less than two hours from the time they ended, the twelve jurors reached their verdict after only a single vote: "We, the jury, find the defendant not guilty."

As the courtroom's audience erupted in cheers, the judge banged his gavel, called for silence, and told the jury of white supremacists, anti-Catholic bigots, and Ku Klux Klansmen, "There will be many opinions, but no one can properly criticize the honest verdict of twelve honest men."

The Klan Welcomes a New Member

Two years later, the darkness of a September evening was illuminated by burning crosses towering over 25,000 people in a Birmingham park. Among the hoods and white robes were 1,500 men moments away from joining the Ku Klux Klan. One of them was Hugo Black.

With the other aspiring "knights" dressed in full Klan regalia, Black marched in a massive circle with military precision. He stopped every 150 yards at one of three ceremonial stations. Finally, his circumnavigation of the flaming crosses completed, Black raised his hand in a Nazi-like salute and repeated the oath of the most deadly and destabilizing hate group in American history.

He swore to "most zealously and valiantly shield and preserve" white supremacy "by any and all justifiable means and methods."

He swore to preserve "the sacred constitutional rights" of "free public schools" and "separation of church and state."[1]

He swore to "never yield to bribery, flattery, passion, punishment, persecution, persuasion, nor any enticements whatever coming or offered to me from any person or persons, male or female, for the purpose of obtaining a secret or secret information of the Ku Klux Klan."

He swore to "die rather than divulge same, so help me God."

And he finished by declaring in unison with his fellow Knights of the Invisible Empire, "All to which I have sworn to by this oath, I will seal with my blood, be thou my witness Almighty God. Amen."

Three years later, due in large part to the network of support he built by delivering anti-Catholic speeches at almost every one of Alabama's 148 Klan "Klaverns," the state of Alabama elected Hugo Black to the U.S. Senate. The state's grand dragon served as his de facto campaign manager.

Eleven years after that, when President Franklin Roosevelt was looking to fill a Supreme Court vacancy with a New Deal southerner who would be easily confirmed by the Senate, he nominated one of the Senate's own: Hugo Black. He was confirmed five days after his nomination was announced in the Senate, with no hearings held and little opposition offered.

It was not until a month later that an investigative reporter sent from Pittsburgh to Alabama paid the Klan's former grand dragon for a set of secret documents with Hugo Black's signature. They proved what had until then only been rumored: To the disgust of many Americans, the newest associate justice of the U.S. Supreme Court had once proudly served in the Ku Klux Klan.[32]

"One More Victory and I Am Undone"

When Black first arrived on the Supreme Court in 1937, he had not practiced law for eleven years. Even when he had been a young up-and-coming lawyer, he had never dealt with complex legal issues. Understandably, Black was far more comfortable grandstanding before a jury (or the Senate) than grappling with the meanings of legal texts and constitutional principles.

Unfortunately for Black, it showed. Justice Harlan Fiske Stone told a reporter on background that Black was, as the journalist paraphrased it in his article, "not a help to his colleagues in the first two or three years." The new justice made "blunders which have shocked his colleagues." He was like a novice tennis player who "had stepped into a fast game" and "ignoring the rules, made vigorous passes at every ball with a piece of board."[33]

Black believed that the Bill of Rights applied to laws passed by state governments. He recognized that the Bill of Rights had originally applied only to the federal government. But in 1868 the nation had ratified the Fourteenth Amendment, which provides, "No State shall make or enforce any law which shall abridge the privileges or immunities of citizens of the United States." Black believed that "the privileges or immunities of citizens" referred to the Bill of Rights.

Few could doubt that Black was at least partially correct. The drafters of the Fourteenth Amendment said they expected it would apply some of the Bill of Rights to the states. Their reference to "the privileges or immunities of citizens" almost certainly encompassed the more fundamental individual rights found in the Bill of Rights, like free speech and due process.

But parts of the Bill of Rights were not individual rights, because parts were intended to protect states, not individuals. It thus made no sense to apply those parts *against* the states. For example, the Tenth Amendment provides, "The powers not delegated to the United States by the Constitution, nor prohibited by it to the States, are reserved to the States respectively, or to the people." The Tenth Amendment could not be applied *against* the states, because its only purpose was to *protect* the states.

The Tenth Amendment was not alone in this regard. The establishment clause was also intended to protect only states, not individuals. As its text and history demonstrate, it offered no protection for individuals. Indeed, over a million individual Americans at the time of ratification lived in states *with* established religions. Instead of protecting *individuals*, the establishment clause insulated *states* against federal interference with their state-established religions.

Nevertheless, by the time Black arrived at the Supreme Court, anti-Catholics wanted to apply the establishment clause against states. They had been waging a war against Catholic schools for nearly a century. In the 1870s Congress had almost passed the Blaine Amendment, which would have prohibited any state from providing any financial support for the education or transportation of children in parochial schools. When the federal statute failed to find enough votes, many states passed their own versions of it. But the nativist lobby continued to long for a federal Blaine Amendment—or the equivalent of it.

By the 1940s, some anti-Catholic activists wanted to make the establishment clause the equivalent of the Blaine Amendment. They wanted to use it to invalidate as unconstitutional any laws that provided funds to Catholic schools. To do so, they needed only to torture its meaning, expand its scope, and apply it against the states it was designed to protect.

In 1947 Hugo Black had an opportunity to do just that. A case arrived at the Supreme Court called *Everson v. Board of Education*. It challenged the constitutionality of a New Jersey statute that allowed school boards to reimburse parents for the costs of their children's transportation to school, including public and parochial schools. The only problem for Black was that at conference, six of his colleagues voted to find the statute constitutional.[34]

Undeterred, Black hatched a plan. By voting with the majority, he would be able to write the majority opinion, which would establish rules binding on legislatures and lower courts. In that opinion, he would apply the establishment clause to the states. And he would interpret the clause to require an unprecedented degree of separation between church and state. Sure, he would have to say that the particular statute in this case did not violate that new principle of separation. But he would be able to establish a principle that could be used against Catholic schools in every court case that came afterward.

Black had long ago sworn before thousands of Klansmen to preserve "the sacred constitutional rights" of "free public schools" and "separation of church and state."[35] Now, twenty-four years later, he vowed to make *Everson* a Pyrrhic victory for the Catholic Church he hated. "'One more victory and I am undone,'" Black said, quoting King Pyrrhus, whose battlefield victory over the Romans came at a crippling cost. "I made it as tight and gave them as little room to maneuver as I could," he later explained.[36]

The result was one of the most transparently misleading and historically inaccurate opinions in Supreme Court history. Black began his analysis by declaring, as if the question had already been decided, that the First Amendment was "made applicable to the states by the Fourteenth."[37] For support, Black cited a single case from four years earlier. But that case, about the constitutional right of Jehovah's Witnesses to proselytize and sell pamphlets door to door, addressed the free exercise clause, an entirely different provision of the First Amendment.

The free exercise clause forbids any law "prohibiting the free exercise" of religion. Unlike the establishment clause—which says, "Congress shall make no law respecting an establishment of religion"—the free exercise clause *does* protect individual rights, because it protects individuals from laws that prohibit the practice of their religion. But this difference did not matter to Hugo Black. Having incorporated the establishment clause against the states in a single sentence, he began to rewrite history to fit his ideological agenda.

The establishment clause, wrote Black, "reflected in the minds of early Americans a vivid mental picture of conditions and practices which they fervently wished to stamp out," in particular the "evils, fears, and political problems" caused by laws establishing religion. Of course, it reflected no such thing. Six of the states that ratified the establishment clause themselves *established* a state religion, and those establishments lasted for decades after the establishment clause was ratified. Comfortable with religious establishment at a state level, the Americans who ratified the Bill of Rights were attempting to prevent the federal government from forcing the various states to accept a single religious denomination.

Nevertheless, Black recast the establishment clause as a protection against religious persecution, rather than a protection of states against federal interference. "A large proportion of the early settlers of this country came here from Europe," where "Catholics had persecuted Protestants, Protestants had persecuted Catholics," sects of each faith had persecuted other sects, and "all of these had from time to time persecuted Jews." This was, of course, true. But as Black's opinion later admitted, European laws establishing religion "were transplanted to" the American colonies. According to Black, they "began to thrive in the soil of the new America."

But establishments of religion did not merely "*beg[i]n* to thrive in the soil of the new America." Establishments of religion endured into the nineteenth century and ended only when John Adams's Massachusetts disestablished state-sponsored religion in 1833—forty-two years after the establishment clause was ratified. Black conveniently rewrote this forty-two-year history and depicted the six states with established religion at the time of ratification as exceptions to the rule.

"These practices," wrote Black, referring to state establishments of religion, "shock[ed] the freedom-loving colonials into a feeling of abhorrence." According to Black, "it was these feelings which found expression in the First Amendment." But he offered not a single citation in support of this supposed insight into the "feelings" of the framers. Black could not provide a solitary piece of historical evidence showing that even one "freedom-loving colonial" believed that the establishment clause applied to states and limited their authority to establish a religion. Nor could Black find any evidence that anyone at the time of the Fourteenth Amendment's ratification intended to transform the establishment clause in this revolutionary manner.

Finally, having incorporated the establishment clause against state and local governments without any support, Black delivered what he hoped would be the coup de grâce for Catholic schools. Not only could states not establish religions; they could have no connection at all to faith-based schools, initiatives, or organizations. The establishment clause, wrote Black, "was intended to erect 'a wall of separation between church and State.'" According to Black, "that wall must be kept high and impregnable. We could not approve the slightest breach."

The phrase "wall of separation" is not found in the First Amendment. Instead, it was coined in an obscure letter written by Thomas Jefferson to a group of Connecticut Baptists, which was rediscovered by Hugo Black. And the problems with Black's misuse of Jefferson's metaphor are fourfold.

First, constitutional provisions require the support of two thirds of each house of Congress and three quarters of the states. They cannot be created by a single letter writer—even one as esteemed as Jefferson—who, in a single line taken from sixty volumes of writings, used a metaphor never proposed, debated, or voted on by the representatives of the American people.[38]

Second, although Black claimed Jefferson played a "leading" role in the "drafting and adoption" of the First Amendment, Thomas Jefferson was actually in France, not Congress, at the time.

Third, Jefferson himself did not govern as if he believed in "a wall of separation between church and State." He believed "no nation has ever yet existed or been governed without religion. Nor can be."[39] He used federal funds to pay the salaries of Catholic priests ministering to American Indians.[40] He also issued Thanksgiving Day proclamations when he was governor of Virginia.

Jefferson did, however, believe that it was monarchical for a national head of state to issue such religious proclamations, and he told his attorney general that the purpose of his reference to a "wall of separation" in his letter to the Baptists was to explain to them "why I do not proclaim fastings and thanksgiving, as my predecessors did."[41]

Fourth and finally, none of Jefferson's contemporaries governed as if a prohibition against a federal establishment of religion required "a wall of separation between church and State." Presidents Washington, Adams, Jefferson, and Madison prayed in their inaugural addresses. Presidents Washington, Adams, and Madison called the nation to fasting and prayer with religious proclamations. George Washington signed into law a statute encouraging federal support of religious schools in the Northwest Territory. The Congress that passed that law—and that wrote the Bill of Rights—opened its sessions with a chaplain's prayer. Courtroom proceedings presided over by Supreme Court justices riding circuit also opened with chaplains' prayers. As Justice Joseph Story wrote in his legendary treatise on the law, "An attempt to level all religions, and to make it a matter of state policy to hold all in utter indifference, would have created universal disapprobation, if not universal indignation."[42]

The role of religion in the public sphere did not escape the notice of Alexis de Tocqueville when he visited the United States in the 1830s. "I do not know whether all Americans put faith in their religion, for who can read into men's hearts?" the Frenchman wrote. "But I am sure that they believe it necessary for the maintenance of republican institutions. This is not an opinion peculiar to one class of citizens or to one party, but to a whole nation; it is found in every rank of society."[43]

This history meant nothing to Justice Black when he wrote *Everson*. Nor did it matter to him the next year, when he authored an opinion in *McCollum v. Board of Education* invalidating a program for a voluntary religious-education class taught on the property of a public school. And for the nearly seventy years since *Everson*, the "wall of separation between church and State" that Black tried to create has been the rallying cry of litigants and legislators who have banned voluntary prayer from schools, the Ten Commandments from courthouses, and crèches from the steps of city halls.

Today, thanks to the Klansman who went from wearing a white

robe to a black robe, the metaphor of "a wall of separation between church and State" is, according to legal scholars, "more familiar to the general public than the Amendment's actual language."[44] Meanwhile, the public is rarely if ever taught that the purpose of the First Amendment's establishment clause was to *protect* states' choices about religion, that the man who casually wrote about "a wall of separation" believed it was constitutional to pay priests with federal funds, and that no less a civil libertarian than John Adams wrote the establishment of religion *into* his state's constitution.

"Mr. Justice, Why Did You Join the Klan?"

Future justices of the Supreme Court like Potter Stewart and Clarence Thomas would later comment on the "irony" of using a constitutional provision designed to *protect* state laws about religion as a weapon to *attack* state laws about religion. But the greater irony in Black's opinion was this: The justice whose opinion in *Everson* defined the relationship between the establishment clause and religious freedom had risen to power on the shoulders of the nation's most dangerous enemy of religious freedom.

For the twenty-four years Black spent on the Court after *Everson*, he continued the assault on the Catholic Church he had begun with his defense of Edwin Stephenson in a Birmingham courtroom. He routinely wrote and joined opinions aimed at undermining support for parochial schools. And when on occasion he was unable to get his way, he reverted to the code words and charged language of his youth. Lashing out in a dissent in 1968, he called those who support aid to religious schools "powerful sectarian religious propagandists . . . looking toward complete domination and supremacy of their particular brand of religion."[45]

One day over lunch in 1958, a law clerk asked out of the blue, "Mr. Justice, why did you join the Klan?"

A painfully awkward silence fell over the lunch table. Clerks rarely ask justices personal questions. They never ask *embarrassing* personal questions.

According to one of the other clerks there, "It was eerie. We just stared straight ahead. Those few seconds seemed like hours."[46]

Then Hugo Black broke the silence. Laughing at his membership in, and reliance on, a terrorist organization responsible for the torture and murder of countless Americans, Black smiled. "Why, son," he said, "if you wanted to be elected to the Senate in Alabama in the 1920s, you'd join the Klan too."

CHAPTER 5

Liberty: "A Reality or a Shadow"?

THE FORGOTTEN FOURTH AMENDMENT

> *The right of the people to be secure in their persons,*
> *houses, papers, and effects, against unreasonable*
> *searches and seizures, shall not be violated, and no*
> *Warrants shall issue, but upon probable cause,*
> *supported by Oath or affirmation, and particularly*
> *describing the place to be searched, and the persons or*
> *things to be seized.*
>
> —UNITED STATES CONSTITUTION, FOURTH AMENDMENT

AT THE TIME OF OUR NATION'S FOUNDING, FEW MEN WERE more admired than the English dissident whom King George III called "that devil Wilkes." A sometime member of Parliament and a sometime political prisoner, John Wilkes argued that the King's subjects had rights, and the King's powers had limits. He spoke out against the king's tyrannical tendencies before there was a Stamp Act, a Boston Tea Party, or a Declaration of Independence. In colonial America, Wilkes's name was synonymous with liberty. The story of how his liberty was won inspired one of the most important parts of our Constitution—the Fourth Amendment.

The Fourth Amendment protects Americans' privacy by, among other things, prohibiting warrants that fail to name the person, place, or things to be searched or seized or that fail to show that there is probable cause to believe that the named target of a search or seizure has committed a crime. The amendment was written to be an ironclad check against one of the worst abuses of King George III—the general warrants that were used by the king's investigators to persecute people like John Wilkes. It should protect the privacy of our personal papers even as we increasingly store them not in desks or filing cabinets but in the cloud and in e-mail. And the amendment should protect us against a recent, high-profile, invasive government program—one involving the sweeping collection and retention of the telephone and e-mail records of hundreds of millions of Americans.

"George, Be King!"

The Prince of Wales had many faults. He was petty. He was stubborn. He was neither unusually perceptive nor particularly intelligent. But even his enemies had to grant him at least one virtue: He was a survivor. Twenty-two years earlier, he had been born two months premature. Now, at his coronation in 1761, the boy whom few had expected to survive past infancy was about to be crowned King George III—ruler of England, Scotland, Wales, Ireland, and royal subjects on five continents, including more than two million loyal colonists stretching from Georgia to New England.

As a boy, George had learned only contempt for the limits imposed on England's monarchs by its Magna Carta, its Bill of Rights, and an unwritten constitution that empowered Parliament to set policy. Raised in isolation by a German mother with little respect for the "rights of Englishmen," the new king heard her favorite instruction in his head when the crown was first placed upon it and in his ears when she repeated it throughout her remaining years: "George," she ordered, "be King!"[1]

Once crowned, the new king wasted no time in attempting to consolidate his power and exert his influence. He used patronage to buy off members of Parliament. He installed a prime minister he could control. He proposed new taxes, particularly an excise tax on cider. And he ended the Seven Years' War he had inherited from his grandfather's reign.

Each of these actions provoked opposition, some of it fierce. The public bristled at the blatant corruption and attempt to dominate Britain's elected representatives. Some regions rioted over the proposed cider tax. Many viewed the peace treaty that ended Britain's war with France as a betrayal of the nation's allies and as a gift to its enemy.

To defend these policies, the government's allies began publishing a "weekly" called the *Briton*. Weeklies were long opinion essays, and they were read by large numbers of the middle class—so many, in fact, that coffeehouses stayed in business by providing copies for customers to read. They staked out fiercely partisan positions in defense of, or in opposition to, the king's ministers, but regardless of their politics, they almost always stopped short of directly criticizing the king. That, of course, was illegal.

Due in part to its politics and in part to its mediocre writing, the *Briton* proved unpopular. But the weekly it inspired to oppose it sold ten times more copies and took the nation by storm. Called the *North Briton*, it ranted against "the infernal doctrine of arbitrary power and indefeasible right on the part of the sovereign."[2] It blasted away at those in government who believed "that the people were made entirely for the sovereign and that he had a right to dispose of their fortunes, lives and liberties."[3] It uncovered fraud, embezzlement, and sweetheart deals. And it mocked the king's ministers: Lord Egremont was "weak, passionate, and insolent";[4] Samuel Martin was "the most treacherous, base, selfish, mean, abject, low-lived and dirty fellow, that ever wriggled himself into a secretaryship";[5] and Lord Bute, the prime minister, "sacrificed the glory and interests of this country to his own private ambition" by making an "inglorious peace" with France.[6]

With every insult aimed at arbitrary power, the *North Briton* gained readers, and with every acid barb, its author gained devotees. Although it was, like most weeklies, written, printed, and funded anonymously, the identity of the essayist behind the *North Briton* was an open secret. He was a young, flamboyant politician with a distinctive squint, an enormous jaw, and a way with words. Within a decade he would become, in the words of William Pitt the elder, "a person of the greatest consequence in the Kingdom."[7] His name was John Wilkes.

Two Stubborn Men

In many ways, John Wilkes was King George's opposite. The son of a distiller, Wilkes had an instinctive connection to those he called, in the era's vernacular for the middle and lower classes, the "middling and inferior class of people." Whereas George saw England's commoners and their representatives in Parliament as an obstacle to his authority, Wilkes saw them as a base of power and fancied himself their natural champion.

Among the biggest differences between Wilkes and his king was Wilkes's ability to coin a phrase or deliver a winning argument. Whereas George's inclination was to lead by the carrot of bribes and stick of executive power, Wilkes quickly learned how to lead through persuasion and the building of political capital. And nothing was more valuable to Wilkes in that strategy than his acerbic wit.

When an opponent predicted Wilkes would die from either hanging or the pox, Wilkes fired back, "That depends, my Lord, on whether I embrace your lordship's principles or your mistress."[8] In an encounter with a voter who told Wilkes he would choose the devil over Wilkes, the candidate replied, "And if your friend decides against standing, can I count on your vote?"[9] On another occasion he toasted to the king's "long life," only to be questioned by his host, the king's son and heir, "Since when have you been so anxious about my parent's health?" Wilkes smiled and said, "Since I had the pleasure of your Royal Highness's acquaintance."[10]

There was, however, a character trait that George III and John Wilkes shared: stubbornness. The king's stubbornness in the face of colonial demands would cost him America. Wilkes's stubbornness would transform constitutional law in Great Britain—and beyond.

"The Sanction of His Sacred Name to the Most Odious Measures"

On the last afternoon of April in 1763—Easter Saturday—John Wilkes sat in the home of Lord Halifax, the king's secretary of state for Britain's Southern Department. Halifax was polite to his fellow member of Parliament, but this was no social call. The secretary of state was a prosecutor, and John Wilkes was under arrest.

Wilkes's latest edition of the *North Briton*—its forty-fifth issue— had excoriated the king's annual address to Parliament, and although it purported to lay blame only with the ministers who wrote the speech, it looked to most readers like a direct rebuke of the king himself.

According to the *North Briton* "Number 45," the king gave "the sanction of his sacred name to the most odious measures," such as the peace with France and the tax on cider. Enforcement of the tax would mean "private houses are now made liable to be entered and searched at pleasure." Playing off the multiple meanings of "prerogative," Wilkes said that the "prerogative of the crown is to exert the constitutional powers entrusted to it," and "freedom is the English subject's prerogative." In his most caustic commentary he said, "I wish as much as any man in the kingdom to see the honor of the crown maintained in a manner truly becoming Royalty. I lament to see it sunk even to prostitution."

For George III, Number 45 was the final straw. He decided that the best way to silence dissent was to make an example out of Wilkes and anyone connected to him. On the king's command, Lord Halifax issued a general warrant authorizing a "strict and diligent search for the authors, printers and publishers of a seditious and treasonable paper entitled, the North Briton Number 45." The warrant called for the king's henchmen to seize "any of them" and their papers.

As soon as Wilkes was shown this warrant, he called it useless. It "named nobody," he said in outrage to Lord Halifax. Warrants, if legal, gave immunity to law enforcement officers against suits for false arrest and trespass on private property, but Wilkes believed they were only entitled to confer immunity if they named a *specific suspect* and were supported by evidence against him. In contrast, a "general warrant" named the crime but not the suspects. Under the auspices of a general warrant, anyone could be dragged from his bed in the dead of night at the whim of the king and held by armed guards without probable cause or even suspicion of having committed a crime.

That was precisely what had happened under the authority of the general warrant presented to Wilkes. Even though Halifax was looking for only three people—the *North Briton* Number 45 had one author, one printer, and one publisher—Wilkes was among the last of forty-nine people arrested under the supposed authority of this single warrant. Many of them—printers and printers' apprentices—had nothing to do with the *North Briton*, and the arrest of these innocents only furthered Wilkes's conviction that the warrant was illegal and invalid.

Halifax questioned Wilkes for a short period of time, but Wilkes—aside from airing his outrage over the general warrant—was unresponsive.

"Am I to understand," asked Halifax, "that you will answer no questions at all?"

"Certainly, my Lord," said Wilkes, "and I thank God I am in a country where there is no torture, and if there was, I hope to have the firmness enough to endure it."

Wilkes would not even answer the question of whether he preferred to be held under house arrest or in prison. "If I am restrained by a superior force, I must yield to the violence," he said, referring to his detention, "but I will never give color to it by a shameful compromise."[11]

Wilkes spent that night—and the next five—in the Tower of London.

"Henceforth Every Innocent Man, However Poor and Unsupported, May Hope to Sleep in Peace and Security in His Own House"

After Wilkes awoke in his prison cell on Easter Sunday, he secured a pen and paper to write on a familiar topic: the deprivation of liberty in King George's England. "As an Englishman," he wrote to his beloved daughter Polly, "I must lament that my liberty is thus wickedly taken away." He lamented that he had "not yet seen my accusers" or even "heard who they are." But, he said, "I am not unhappy, for my honor is clear, and my health good, and my spirit unshaken, I believe indeed, invincible." He added that "the most pleasing thoughts I have are of you."[12]

That same day, protesters paraded through the streets of London, led by members of Parliament allied with Wilkes. Those from the House of Commons rode on horseback. Nobles rode in carriages.

Lawyers, printers, and men of business joined in the march, while ballads were sung by commoners in Wilkes's honor and his face was painted on tavern signs across London.

By Friday, when Wilkes was taken from the Tower of London to Westminster Hall for his habeas corpus hearing, countless commoners ran alongside his carriage shouting support. They then packed the balcony of the courtroom until they overflowed into the streets, waiting to hear word of Wilkes's argument and of the judge's decision.

Wilkes did not disappoint. Standing before the dais of Lord Chief Justice Pratt, who wore a black robe and a long white wig, the dissident declared that more was at stake than his own freedom. "The liberty of all peers and gentlemen—and, what touches me more sensibly, that of all the middling and inferior set of people, who stand most in need of protection—is, in my case, this day to be finally decided upon." The question was "whether English liberty be a reality or a shadow."[13]

With the audience in the balcony hanging on his every word, Wilkes said he had suffered "imprisonment, the effect of premeditated malice." He had received word that his house had been "ransacked and plundered" by the king's men, "my most private and secret concerns divulged." This was "tyranny," which he trusted would "be finally extirpated" by the court today, so that "henceforth every innocent man, however poor and unsupported, may hope to sleep in peace and security in his own house, unviolated by the king's messengers, and the arbitrary mandates of an overbearing secretary of state."[14]

No one doubted that Wilkes's words inspired his acolytes in the balcony, but when he finished, their effect on the judge whose decision mattered remained unclear. Lord Chief Justice Pratt was not known as an enemy of liberty, but was he prepared to side with Wilkes and defy his king?

In the end, Pratt opted to exploit something of a technicality within the law. He ruled that "parliamentary privilege" required Wilkes's release from prison. It was hardly a decision that provided protection for the "innocent man" who hoped "to sleep in peace and security in his own house." But for the moment, Wilkes's admirers saw plenty to celebrate. Their hero was free.

When Wilkes turned and bowed to his fans, they erupted into cheers and applause, and their celebrations quickly created chaos in and out of the courtroom. Like a celebrity, Wilkes was followed by thousands of Englishmen through the streets. Shouts of "Wilkes and liberty!" rang throughout London and continued into an evening when skies were illuminated by bonfires in Wilkes's honor.

Before long, copies of Wilkes's arguments in the courtroom were printed in allied newspapers and read by thousands throughout England. According to one of his biographers, the hero's "image could be found on tobacco papers, halfpenny ballads, porcelain dishes, punch-bowls, teapots, prints and broadsides." Across the country "there was hardly a workingman who did not believe that Wilkes was the only man who would stand up for him; dissenters almost to a man were ready to serve him; small businessmen, farmers, lawyers, virtually all of the middle classes found hope in the audacious challenges to authority."[15]

Wilkes's six days in prison had transformed a protester into a folk legend. But his greatest triumphs—and their effect on the Constitution of an as-yet-unimagined nation—were still to come.

"The Security of My Own House, the Liberty of My Person, and Every Right of the People"

John Wilkes returned home from prison on the evening of May 6, 1763, to a house raided by Halifax's henchmen. Locks on doors and desk drawers had been broken off. Hinges had been torn down. Papers had been ripped from inside desks and flung with books across the floor. Anything related to the *North Briton* was gone, as was Wilkes's pocketbook. Because Halifax's general warrant included no specifics about who could be seized or what papers could be searched, it had in effect authorized a fishing expedition inside Wilkes's home—and inside the home and office of any of the other forty-eight men arrested without probable cause.

Wilkes was exhausted from a day that had begun in prison, proceeded to court, and culminated with celebrations in the streets, but his energy was far from spent. He immediately wrote to Lord Halifax and another secretary of state noting that his house had been "robbed" and insisting that "the stolen goods" in their possession be returned to him "forthwith." When the executive officials replied the next day that "evidence" would be held for "prosecution," Wilkes told them he feared "neither your prosecution nor your persecution." He promised to continue to "assert the security of my own house, the liberty of my person, and every right of the people, not so much for my own sake, as for the sake of every one of my English fellow subjects."[16]

A week later, Wilkes filed a lawsuit against Halifax and three other officials. The action alleged that the government officials had illegally trespassed in his home, violated his privacy, and damaged his property. Its outcome would depend on the legality of the general warrant that purported to authorize each of those alleged torts.

"A Right, Under Precedent, to Force Persons' Houses"

Seven months later, on December 6, Wilkes stood once again before Lord Chief Justice Pratt and the high dais in Westminster Hall. Once more the gallery was packed with throngs of adoring followers. But this time Wilkes was not defending himself; he was accusing His Majesty's government of wrongdoing and demanding thousands of pounds in damages.

In addition, this time Wilkes had the benefit of a jury—"twelve good men and true."[17] Jurors tended to be drawn from London's business class, and Wilkes knew that these commoners were over-whelmingly on his side. They looked shocked when witnesses testi-fied about the twenty doors in Wilkes's home that had been pried open by government officials. They were outraged that officials had rifled through Wilkes's most private papers for twelve hours. They were liberty-loving Englishmen who felt as a friend of Wilkes had felt when an officer had asked him on the night of the search to bear witness to the seizure of certain papers: "What you are doing," he said, "is too barbarous an act for any human eye to witness."

There was one man, however, who had the potential to render the jury powerless: Lord Chief Justice Pratt. If he ruled that the general warrant signed by Lord Halifax was legal, then the search would be legal as a matter of law, and the jury would not be allowed to award Wilkes any damages.

When the moment of decision came, Wilkes and his supporters in the balcony fixed their eyes on the judge with rapt attention. At first, Lord Pratt did not tip his hand. Instead, he summarized the government's argument—that it had "a right, under precedent, to force persons' houses, break open escritoires, seize their papers, upon a general warrant" in which "no offenders' names are specified." This would mean "a discretionary power" of the state's messengers "to search wherever their suspicions may chance to fall."[18]

Finally, Pratt made his opinion clear: "If such a power is truly vested in a secretary of state, and he can delegate this power, it cer-tainly may affect . . . every man in this kingdom and is totally sub-versive of the liberty of the subject."[19] With those words and the ruling that followed, Pratt had not only invalidated the warrant in Wilkes's case; he had outlawed *all* general warrants in all future cases.

Freed by the judge to reach any verdict it wished, the jury ruled for Wilkes in spectacular fashion. Lord Halifax was forced to pay Wilkes £4,000.[20] Moreover, Wilkes encouraged suits from twenty-five printers and apprentices who had been subjected to arrests and searches under Halifax's general warrant. Their verdicts cost the British government around £100,000—over $13 million in today's value.[21]

The result of the suits was a jolt to England's unwritten constitution. General warrants that named a crime but no criminals had been the last remnant of an era before the Magna Carta when "divinely inspired" monarchs wielded absolute power over English subjects.[22] They allowed the king to invade any home, seize any person, and search any papers—all without probable cause or anything approaching due process. But now, after Wilkes's victory spelled their demise, England truly was a *constitutional* monarchy. "Every innocent man" could, in Wilkes's words, "sleep in peace and security in his own house, unviolated by the king's messengers, and the arbitrary mandates of an overbearing secretary of state."[23]

That afternoon, the people of London unleashed a new cheer outside Wilkes's house: "Pratt, Wilkes, and liberty for ever!"[24]

The "Phoenix"

In the years after his victory in court, Wilkes continued to oppose King George's corrupt practices, autocratic style, and foolish policies. In turn, the king continued to try to silence him. He prosecuted Wilkes for publishing an indecent poem and for republishing the *North Briton* Number 45. The allies he had bought off in Parliament expelled Wilkes from the House of Commons. The king's judges convicted Wilkes of seditious and salacious libel. His jailers imprisoned Wilkes for nearly two years. His soldiers fired into crowds of Wilkes's rambunctious supporters and massacred them at a place called St. George's Fields.

But every attack on Wilkes backfired on the crown and magnified the political prisoner's image as a martyr for freedom. After each of five expulsions from the House of Commons, the voters returned Wilkes to Parliament, sometimes within a fortnight of his expulsion—even though, during three of those elections, he was in prison. Wilkes was also elected alderman in 1769, sheriff in 1771, and mayor of London in 1774. In that same year he was reelected to Parliament and finally, for the first time since he had written Number 45, not expelled.

Throughout those years, Wilkes's hordes of admirers expressed their enthusiasm in a multitude of ways—many of them benign; some of them humorous; a few of them violent. Supporters sent him two thousand pounds of gifts while he was in prison. Audiences at the theater and the racetrack called out to George III, "Wilkes and liberty!" The number "45" was scratched on thousands of coaches, doors, and windows. On Wilkes's birthday, crowds sang, "God save great Wilkes our king!"

On other nights dedicated to Wilkes, every house in London was lit with candles—even those of the king's aunt and brother, who knew their windows would be smashed by mobs if they didn't join in honoring Wilkes. A visiting Benjamin Franklin reported that fifty thousand pounds of candles had been used to celebrate Wilkes in just two nights after one of his elections and that "for fifteen miles out of town there was not a door or window shutter next to the road unmarked" with the number that had become a symbol of Wilkes and liberty—45. Londoners even dragged the Austrian ambassador from his coach and used chalk to write "45" on the bottom of his shoes. On multiple occasions—sometimes in celebration of Wilkes's victories, sometimes in protest against his persecution—his supporters rioted.

One indication of Wilkes's popularity was the public's treatment of a printer who had been sentenced to the pillory for the crime of printing the *North Briton*. It was not unheard of for a criminal in the pillory to be stoned to death by mobs. But the crowd around the printer who published the *North Briton* didn't harm him at all. Instead, they chanted "Wilkes and liberty" while he was in the pillory and then gave him two hundred guineas as a reward for his courage.

Even George III's own young children caught the Wilkes fever. They sometimes opened the door to their father's room and cried, "Wilkes and Number 45 forever!"[25]

Perhaps Horace Walpole, a politician and the son of Britain's first prime minister, said it best when he called Wilkes a "phoenix" upon his election as sheriff. Wilkes, said Walpole, waged "a war against a King, ministers, courts of law, a whole legislature, and all Scotland," which was a royalist region. "His colleagues betray him, desert him, expose him, and he becomes sheriff of London. I believe if he was to be hanged, he would be made King of England."[26]

"I Believe in Wilkes, the Firm Patriot, Maker of Number 45"

During this eleven-year period of persecution of John Wilkes, antipathy for King George III and demands for the "rights of Englishmen" were growing rapidly in the American colonies. In 1761 writs of assistance provoked outrage by, like general warrants, permitting British officials to search any American's home or business. In 1765 the Stamp Act led to cries of "no taxation without representation." In 1767 a tax on imports from Britain to the colonies led to a boycott of British goods. In 1770 British soldiers killed five civilians in the Boston Massacre. In 1773 a new tax on tea led to the most famous tea party in history. The next year, in 1774, Britain's "Intolerable Acts" closed Boston's port; eliminated colonists' control over Massachusetts's local government; allowed British soldiers guilty of murder in the colonies to be tried back home in Britain; and established a new regime for quartering the king's occupying army.

In the midst of rising outrage against King George's army, his removal of cases from American juries, and his unconstitutional taxation, John Wilkes's (literal) trials and famous tribulations at the hands of the king did not go unnoticed in the American colonies. His liberty, like that of the colonists, was under attack. His home had been searched, just as their homes had been searched. His voters' elections had been nullified by his expulsions from Parliament, just as colonists' elections had been nullified by decrees shutting down colonial legislatures. His writings had led to charges of seditious libel, just as Patriots' writings had led to prosecutions for seditious libel. His unarmed supporters had been killed by soldiers at St. George's Fields, just as unarmed colonists had been killed by soldiers at the Boston Massacre.

As a result, Wilkes became a cult figure in the colonies. A creed was written and published in Boston based on the Apostles' Creed; it began, "I believe in Wilkes, the firm patriot, maker of number 45. Who was born for our good. Suffered under arbitrary power. Was banished and imprisoned."[27] Elsewhere in the colonies, Wilkes was honored by the naming of Wilkes County, Georgia; Wilkesboro, North Carolina; and Wilkes-Barre, Pennsylvania.

At the center of Wilkes's cult following was an obsession with the number forty-five, which became a symbol for resistance to royal tyranny as universally recognized in America as it was in Britain. Forty-five hogsheads of tobacco were sent to Wilkes from Virginia and Maryland. Forty-five toasts to celebrate Wilkes's release from prison were drunk by Club Forty-Five in South Carolina, at a meeting that began at seven forty-five and ended at twelve forty-five. Forty-five New Yorkers joined an imprisoned pamphleteer named Alexander McDougall in jail, and together they ate forty-five pounds of steak cut from a forty-five-month-old bull on the forty-fifth day of the year. Forty-five virgins sang McDougall forty-five songs on the same day, although someone "dismissed the incident by saying all the virgins were forty-five years old."[28]

Even the judge who ruled in Wilkes's case that general warrants were invalid found fame and admiration in America. Soon after his decision in Wilkes's case, Lord Chief Justice Pratt inherited the title Lord Camden. As in Camden, New Jersey. And Camden, South Carolina. And the B&O Railroad's Camden Station, on whose rail yards was later built the home of the Baltimore Orioles—Camden Yards.

But John Wilkes's real significance to the American experiment isn't found in the names of cities or baseball parks. It is found in the words of the Fourth Amendment of the United States Constitution and in the principle of privacy from government intrusion and surveillance that the amendment was designed to protect.

An Englishman Inspires America's Fourth Amendment

By the time James Madison began drafting the Bill of Rights in 1789, no case was more famous in America than John Wilkes's trespass suit against Lord Halifax and his messengers. Its "plot and cast of characters were familiar to every schoolboy in America."[29] It was "*the* paradigmatic search and seizure case for Americans."[30]

The lessons Americans drew from Wilkes's case were relatively straightforward. A man's house was private. So were his papers. Only a tyrannical government could invade that privacy by searching his property without just cause and meaningful limits. The best protection against such tyranny was to prohibit general warrants, which named the alleged crime but not the location of the search or the identity of the suspected criminal. If a warrant were going to immunize investigators—as was occasionally necessary—the warrant required evidence of probable cause that the target of the search had committed a crime.

During the debates over ratifying the Constitution, Americans of all political persuasions—Federalists and Anti-Federalists—understood those lessons and cherished the man whose case had embodied them. But Anti-Federalists went further. They wanted those lessons enshrined in the text of the Constitution.

An Anti-Federalist essay by the "Maryland Farmer" was typical. "Suppose for instance, that an officer of the United States should force the house, the asylum of a citizen, by virtue of a general warrant," he wrote. "Are general warrants illegal by the Constitution of the United States?"[31] He doubted it. And he doubted that liberty could survive in the United States unless an explicit prohibition against general warrants was added to the Constitution.

So many other Americans agreed—not just about the need to add to the Constitution explicit guarantees against unreasonable searches and general warrants but also about the need to protect other fundamental rights—that Federalists promised to add a Bill of Rights to the Constitution if it was ratified.

James Madison kept that promise in 1789 when he drafted the Bill of Rights and introduced it in the First Congress. Madison's proposal protected from federal interference the bundle of rights that Americans most cherished, and at the center of those protections was the Fourth Amendment: "The right of the people to be secure in their persons, houses, papers, and effects, against unreasonable searches and seizures, shall not be violated, and no Warrants shall issue, but upon probable cause, supported by Oath or affirmation, and particularly describing the place to be searched, and the persons or things to be seized."

Its text was as clear as the lessons from John Wilkes's story: Warrants must describe "the place to be searched." They must name the "person or things to be seized." There must be "probable cause" to support those warrants.

In short, broad warrants purporting to give government agents discretion to rummage through the homes and private papers of law-abiding Americans—*i.e.*, general warrants—are incompatible with liberty. And under the Fourth Amendment, they are unconstitutional.

Nevertheless, for at least the past eight years, the federal government has relied on an excessively broad interpretation of an excessively broad provision of the USA PATRIOT Act (usually called simply the PATRIOT Act) to collect and, in some circumstances, search through vast amounts of information that most Americans would consider both private and entirely unrelated to national security. While experts may disagree as to whether the government's recent practices can fairly be described as the information-age equivalent of general warrants, I believe they dangerously undermine the core interests protected by the Fourth Amendment and infringe on the liberty defended by John Wilkes and championed by his American admirers.[32]

A Simple Question

In the summer of 2012, the director of national intelligence, James Clapper, sat beside five other executive-branch officials at a rare open hearing of the Senate Intelligence Committee. The seventy-one-year-old Clapper had spent a lifetime in the intelligence community, much of it while wearing an air force uniform. A retired general, he had served his nation with distinction during a career spent trying to keep America safe. But on this day, at this hearing, he made a mistake.

Toward the end of the hearing, Oregon's Senator Ron Wyden asked Clapper a simple question. "Does the NSA collect any type of data at all on millions or hundreds of millions of Americans?"

It has never been a secret that the National Security Agency collects vast amounts of digital data on *foreign* threats to the United States. In fact, *every 14.4 seconds* it adds to its collection the same quantity of information that is in the Library of Congress.[33] The agency recently built a $1.5 billion electronic warehouse in Utah, just to keep up with its ever-growing data-storage needs.

But Senator Wyden's question wasn't about foreign intelligence. He wanted to know whether the NSA collects data "on millions or hundreds of millions of *Americans*."

In response, Clapper could not have looked less comfortable. He stared down toward his lap, resting his head on the tips of his fingers. He had sworn an oath that day to tell the truth, and he now had to decide how to respond.

"No, sir," he said, raising his head to peer quickly at the senator before quickly looking back down.

"It does not?" asked Senator Wyden.

"Not wittingly," said Clapper, who by now was nervously scratching and shaking his head. "There are cases where they could inadvertently, perhaps, but not wittingly."

The director of national intelligence had just been asked to tell the American people whether their government was spying on them, and he had made his decision. He answered that question in the negative. There was, however, a problem with that answer: It wasn't accurate.

An "Indiscriminate and Arbitrary Invasion"

Less than three months later, the world learned the shocking truth. Since as far back as late 2001, the federal government has required mobile telephone companies to turn over to the NSA their customers' call records. The vast majority of these records relate to purely domestic calls in which both participants are located in the United States. The records include every number each customer called, the numbers of everyone who called the customer, the time of day that every call occurred, and the duration of every call. The NSA compiles these records and retains them for up to five years.

Hundreds of millions of Americans have therefore had their calling data collected by the NSA not because they have made phone calls *to suspected terrorists* but simply because they have . . . well . . . made phone calls. It is important to keep in mind that the overwhelming majority of them have committed no crime and have otherwise done *nothing* to raise the suspicions of those charged with protecting the United States from attack. Nevertheless, federal authorities have interpreted a section of the PATRIOT Act to authorize the NSA and the FBI to obtain what some might consider the information-age equivalent of a general warrant, enabling government agents to search though the phone records of hundreds of millions of innocent Americans. The act says the government can ask a specialized tribunal called the Foreign Intelligence Surveillance Court, which meets in secret and which hears only from the government, to order companies like Verizon to turn over records if the records are "relevant" for "an investigation . . . to protect against international terrorism."[34]

If you think the NSA doesn't consider *your* phone records "relevant" to a terrorism investigation, think again.

Here's what the FISA Court secretly authorized the NSA to do. First, it may collect—and we now know that it has in fact collected—hundreds of millions of phone records, which it then retains in a massive database. Second, it may search for a phone number with a suspected connection to terrorism. Third, it may look at every number the suspect's number called and every number from which it received calls. Fourth, it may look at every number that those numbers called and from which they received calls. And finally, it may take all those numbers and poke around—trying to learn anything it can that might help in an investigation.

A federal judge recently illustrated the extent of this multiple-degrees-of-separation searching.[35] Imagine that the NSA finds the number (123) 456-7890 suspicious. Now imagine that (123) 456-7890 called, or was called by, one hundred numbers over five years—an exceptionally conservative estimate. Next imagine that each of those one hundred numbers called or was called by one hundred other numbers.

If you have one of the ten thousand phone numbers in this single query, the NSA may have deemed itself authorized to collect and potentially analyze every number you called and every number that called you, as well as the time, date, and duration of your every call. Taken alone, that might not be a staggering amount of information. But when taken together and analyzed, it can be disturbingly revealing. With it, the government can paint a startlingly clear picture of you—from your politics to your faith to your most intimate relationships.[36]

Those who defend this program are quick to point out that it involves only the collection of data points and that this particular program does not involve the collection of the contents (i.e., the words spoken) of the phone calls in question. That, however, overlooks factors related to the efficiency with which this kind of data can be aggregated and analyzed on a massive scale. The contents of a phone call are generally far more difficult to analyze than the data related to an individual's calling records. That difficulty places some inherent limitations on the government's ability to invade the privacy of the citizenry. Many of those limitations are minimized (or even eliminated altogether) in the case of data. That may be good news for the government, but it could be bad news for Americans who are concerned about their privacy.

The extent of the private information the government can glean from this data is severely magnified by the intensity of the relationship that many, perhaps most, Americans have with their cellular phones. Over 90 percent of American adults have a mobile phone. They spend 2.3 trillion minutes per year talking on them.

If you have any doubt about what the government can learn from your call records, take a moment to scroll through the call history on the cellular phone that is most likely within an arm's length of you right now. After that, try to picture what the call history would look like if it went back *five years*.[37] Finally, consider the unconfirmed reports that the telephone data collected by the NSA sometimes contains information about *where you were* when the calls were placed.[38]

With five years' worth of that information, the NSA can know more about many phone-carrying Americans than most of their friends and families know. As explained by Judge Richard Leon of the United States District Court for the District of Columbia, it is impossible to "imagine a more indiscriminate and arbitrary invasion than this systematic and high-tech collection and retention of personal data on virtually every single citizen for purposes of querying and analyzing it without prior judicial approval." He also noted "the utter lack of evidence that a terrorist attack has ever been prevented because searching the NSA database was faster than other investigative tactics."[39] Instead, the only thing the NSA has to show for its program are countless violations of privacy as profound as those authorized by the general warrants of John Wilkes's era.

"My Response Was Clearly Erroneous"

The day after the NSA's data-collection program was revealed by a British newspaper, the director of national intelligence continued his obfuscation. Director Clapper told the *National Journal*, "What I said was, the NSA does not voyeuristically pore through U.S. citizens' emails. I stand by that."[40] That, of course, is not at all what he said at the Senate hearing.

Two days after that, he still refused to admit that he had failed to answer Senator Wyden's question accurately. "I thought though in retrospect I was asked [a] 'when are you going to stop beating your wife' kind of question, meaning not answerable necessarily, by a simple yes or no," he told NBC's Andrea Mitchell. "So I responded in what I thought was the most truthful, or least untruthful manner, by saying, 'No.' "[41]

Only later, in a letter to the chairwoman of the Senate Intelligence Committee, did Clapper admit the obvious. "My response," he wrote, "was clearly erroneous."[42]

"If Men Were Angels. . . ."

With this power to snoop (including not only the technological capability but also the claimed authority) comes the patently frightening potential to pry into Americans' private lives for purposes *other than national security*. Some NSA agents have already been caught spying on girlfriends they suspected of infidelity.[43] One can easily imagine how other rogue agents could abuse this power for other illicit purposes. One could argue, however, that the far greater threat to government of the people, by the people, and for the people is the near certainty that those who wield this power will eventually use it to identify and punish anyone who may disagree with them. This type of abuse could weaken or even destroy constitutionally limited government as we know it.

As Americans, we know all too well that corrupt regimes like King George III's have a natural tendency to do everything they can to *maintain* power and, where possible, *expand* it. There is no more effective (if diabolical) way of doing this than by silencing voices of dissent—not through the art of persuasion but through the intimidating, often-unrivaled power of government. Unfortunately, this kind of abuse did not end with the Revolutionary War, the drafting of the Constitution, or the ratification of the Fourth Amendment.

There is disturbing modern precedent for *exactly* this type of abuse. A report issued in 1976 by the so-called Church Committee—a select committee of senators commissioned to investigate the intelligence activities of the United States government—found shocking levels of abuse. In the 1960s and '70s, federal agents spied on high-profile and controversial figures and everyday Americans alike. The government spied on reporters for the *New York Times* and the *Washington Post*. It listened in on the phone calls of antiwar Americans—groups, activists, and even senators.[44] And it conducted domestic surveillance on controversial public figures like Martin Luther King Jr. and Muhammad Ali.

But it didn't stop there. The government conducted surveillance of hundreds of thousands of Americans. According to the Church Report, the FBI maintained files on a staggering *one million* Americans between 1960 and 1974, investigating 500,000 supposed "subversives."[45]

The spying was hardly innocuous. The Church Committee found that the government had targeted Americans, often using invasive techniques including bugs, wiretaps, and home invasions. Targets were frequently singled out based on their political convictions, regardless of whether they exhibited an inclination toward dangerous or illegal behavior. According to the Church Committee, since FDR, presidential administrations of both political parties had "permitted, and sometimes encouraged, government agencies to handle essentially political intelligence."[46]

As much as I would like to believe that this kind of abuse will never occur again in America, human nature and history tell us that it will—that is, absent a reinvigoration of the Fourth Amendment and the principles underlying it. The well-known tendency of those in power to engage in it is why so many Americans instinctively distrust big government. Sure, many people in power are law abiding and well meaning. In fact, let's assume here that the *overwhelming majority* of them are. But not everyone is. Once government has the tools to abuse power, it is only a matter of time before someone will do so.

Anyone looking for current examples of this tendency to abuse power need look no further than the current administration—and by that I mean not just the Obama administration but any administration in power at any time. Sometimes that tendency can be seen in the Oval Office itself. More often, however, it shows up in far less prominent positions of power; presidents are generally far more measured with their words than many who serve under them. That makes it far more disturbing when the commander in chief himself shows symptoms of this human frailty.

It remains unclear what President Obama meant when he announced, shortly before the 2010 midterm elections, "We're gonna punish our enemies, and we're gonna reward our friends." But given the immense power that he wields, it is unsettling.

Regardless of what he might have intended, it is easy to understand why some with access to the levers of government—including many who might not even know him or have access to him—might view such a statement as a set of political marching orders. We later learned, of course, that starting in 2010, the IRS began punishing conservative nonprofit organizations by delaying and denying them the tax-exempt status to which they were entitled. And when the agency was called out on this, it then suspiciously (and ironically) "lost" years' worth of e-mails that might have shed light on who was criminally responsible.

Because of the ability to collect vast amounts of information about Americans' private lives, the NSA's domestic spying makes it all too easy for the government to identify political opponents for harassment. That may take the form of embarrassing them, extorting them, framing them, or prosecuting them. Those who doubt that this will eventually happen should recall the very reason we have a government of limited powers and checks and balances—

"government itself," in the words of *Federalist 51*, is "the greatest of all reflections on human nature. If men were angels, no government would be necessary. If angels were to govern men, neither external nor internal controls on government would be necessary."

"Arbitrary Invasions by Government Officials"

The Fourth Amendment's prohibition against general warrants is one of the "controls" that the founding generation demanded that the Constitution impose on the government. According to the Supreme Court, the "basic purpose of this Amendment, as recognized in countless decisions of this Court, is to safeguard the privacy and security of individuals against arbitrary invasions by government officials."[47]

It was the invasion of John Wilkes's "privacy and security" that led to his arrest and later inspired the Fourth Amendment. It's worth considering the multitude of similarities between, on the one hand, general warrants like the one used to search the papers of John Wilkes and, on the other hand, the domestic spying program that is used to search the telephone and e-mail records of Americans today. Like general warrants, the NSA's program covers everyone—not just those suspected of a crime. Like general warrants, the NSA's program allows the government to search first and name suspects later. Like general warrants, the NSA's program allows the government to learn about your politics, your religion, your business affairs, and the identities of your closest friends and family. Like general warrants, the NSA's program relies on orders issued in secret. Like general warrants, the NSA's programs afford innocent people no opportunity to challenge the government's decision to invade their privacy.

Whether it is an eighteenth-century general warrant or a twenty-first-century collection of metadata, a fishing expedition through the records of innocent people's private records violates citizens' privacy, invites partisan persecution, and threatens liberty. The defense of that principle was among the reasons Patriots fought and bled on battlefields from Lexington to Yorktown. And only our insistence on that principle will, in Wilkes's words, make the liberty given to us by God—and protected by the Fourth Amendment—a "reality," rather than a "shadow."

CHAPTER 6

"But Structure Means Liberty"

THE FORGOTTEN TENTH AMENDMENT
AND THE INFLATED COMMERCE CLAUSE

> *The powers not delegated to the United States by the*
> *Constitution, nor prohibited by it to the States, are*
> *reserved to the States respectively, or to the people.*
>
> —UNITED STATES CONSTITUTION, TENTH AMENDMENT

> *The Congress shall have Power . . . to regulate*
> *Commerce with foreign Nations, and among the several*
> *States, and with the Indian Tribes.*
>
> —UNITED STATES CONSTITUTION, ARTICLE I, SECTION 8

AT THE TIME OF THE CONSTITUTION'S DRAFTING AND RATIFI-
cation, state legislatures had the power to pass laws covering almost
every imaginable policy area. They could regulate land use, set re-
quirements for public schools, and criminalize anything from arson
to horse stealing. This open-ended authority to regulate was known
as the "police power."

When the Constitution's drafters created the federal government, they decided *not* to give it this general "police power." Federal powers would be limited. Congress was authorized to enact laws with respect to a relatively small number of topics, nearly all of which are listed in the eighth section of the Constitution's first article. The understanding of the framers was that if a particular power was not granted to Congress in the Constitution, Congress could not exercise that power. This was the reason Madison argued for so long that a bill of rights was not necessary.

During the debate over the Constitution's ratification, skeptics questioned whether Congress would try to expand its powers beyond those enumerated in that document. In effect, they said: *Sure, the Constitution lists only a small number of areas over which Congress can legislate. But what about the unlisted areas? The Constitution doesn't explicitly say Congress can't pass laws about them too.*

Defenders of the Constitution, known as Federalists, were quick to say that the Constitution did not need to explicitly prohibit Congress from passing laws with respect to powers not listed as federal in that document. The text of the Constitution made clear that Congress was an institution with limited, enumerated powers. It would, for example, have made little sense to grant Congress the power to enact laws protecting copyrights and patents or establishing a uniform system of weights and measures if the Constitution had granted Congress broad, open-ended power, analogous to the power possessed by the state legislatures.

But the Constitution's skeptics, known as Anti-Federalists, remained unsatisfied by the logic of the Federalists, so the Federalists agreed to an amendment that would state explicitly what the Constitution's enumeration of Congress's powers already implied: Congress's powers are not unlimited; Congress may exercise only the relatively few powers identified as federal by the Constitution.

That clarification became the Tenth Amendment, concluding the Bill of Rights with an important, if somewhat obvious, statement about the limited nature of Congress's powers: "The powers not delegated to the United States by the Constitution, nor prohibited by it to the States, are reserved to the States respectively, or to the people."

For most of our nation's history, Congress respected the limits on its powers embodied in the Tenth Amendment. But over time, advocates for more federal control over our lives began to promote a radical interpretation of the Constitution. According to them, there are no limits on Congress's power.

Their argument goes like this: because (1) the Constitution's "commerce clause" (Article I, Section 8, Clause 3) gives Congress the power to regulate "commerce . . . among the several states," and because (2) almost everything affects "commerce . . . among the several states," (3) Congress can regulate almost everything.

In the past eight decades, this theory has risen to previously unimaginable heights. By forgetting the Tenth Amendment and expanding the commerce clause beyond all recognition, the theory's advocates have subverted the most important of the Constitution's foundational principles: the federal government's powers are limited, not open-ended.

In the early days of the republic, President Andrew Jackson not only understood this foundational principle; he also acted on it. When Congress passed a bill he deemed outside of its enumerated powers, he did not choose to sign the bill, hoping that the Supreme Court would eventually invalidate it as unconstitutional. Jackson vetoed it—in open defiance of any political costs that the bill's supporters might impose.

A century later, President Franklin Roosevelt took a different approach to limitations on federal powers; he ignored them. Roosevelt believed the federal government was empowered by the Constitution to do anything he deemed to be in the best interests of the nation, regardless of whether the authority to legislate on certain matters had been reserved for the states. Roosevelt asserted that the federal government was empowered to meet "each and every problem" with "a national character," especially those problems that in his view "could not be met by merely local action." He invited the Supreme Court to adopt his vision of an omnipotent federal government and abandon its defense of the Constitution. Fearing the president's threat to pack the Court, they caved.

Nearly eight decades after that, a new president offered the Supreme Court the same invitation.

And once again, instead of returning the nation to its founding principles, the Supreme Court accepted his invitation.

"I Should Have Hit Him If He Had Shot Me Through the Brain"

Young Charles Dickinson was rich, charismatic, and the best shot in Tennessee. As he rode north from Nashville to dueling grounds in Kentucky, he and his entourage of friends were happy and boastful. There was no doubt in their minds that the twenty-seven-year-old Dickinson would win tomorrow's duel.

At several stops along the road, the cocky Dickinson pulled out his pistol and shot right through a string eight yards away. "If General Jackson comes along this road," Dickinson told an innkeeper with whom he left a split string, "show him *that!*"[1]

The trip north was an altogether different one for Dickinson's opponent, General Andrew Jackson. Though comfortable around guns and cool under fire, Jackson was not nearly as quick or as accurate with a pistol as Dickinson. The nearly forty-year-old Jackson had little to boast about and much to fear as he and his second—General Thomas Overton—traveled toward the appointed spot. So, rather than shooting at string, Jackson and Overton talked strategy. Only with a clever plan and a lot of guts would Andrew Jackson have any chance of surviving to see the sunset tomorrow.

Jackson had not wanted this fight. But he had done little to avoid it. Both he and Dickinson had taken to the pages of a local newspaper to air their grievances over a misunderstanding about money. Each had called the other a liar, and somewhere along the line, while drunk, Dickinson had insulted the honor of Jackson's beloved wife. Jackson called Dickinson a "base poltroon and cowardly talebearer." Dickinson called Jackson a "worthless scoundrel, a poltroon and a coward." In 1806 these were fighting words.

At the appointed hour, Jackson and Dickinson stared at each other from eights paces apart, each holding a loaded pistol at his side.

Overton asked, "Are you ready?"

"I am ready," answered Dickinson, still as confident as ever.

"I am ready," answered Jackson, sure that he had devised a foolproof plan of attack.

"Fire!" called Overton.

A single shot rang out. Dust erupted from Jackson's coat. He gritted his teeth. With his empty hand, he clenched his chest.

Everyone there except Jackson and Overton stood wide-eyed in disbelief. They knew Dickinson could not have missed his shot. But how was Jackson still standing?

"Great God!" shouted Dickinson. "Have I missed him?"

"Back to the mark, sir!" Overton ordered Dickinson, who had taken a step back. Overton knew that Jackson had planned to let Dickinson fire first. He knew that Jackson had calculated that he would never win a contest that depended on firing both fast and straight. Only if Jackson had the chance to take his time and steady his aim did he have any chance of hitting Dickinson.

Now, with what seemed like all the time in the world to take aim at a defenseless Dickinson, that is exactly what Jackson did. Full of pain from the bullet that was lodged inches from his heart, Jackson raised his gun, aimed it at Dickinson's chest, and fired.

Dickinson died that day of the wound inflicted by Jackson's slow-but-steady shot. Jackson lived another thirty-nine years. In all that time, Jackson carried inside his chest the bullet Dickinson had fired there—the cost of a strategy that had saved Jackson's life and a symbol of every one of Jackson's virtues and vices: his courage; his cleverness; his inflexibility; his penchant for violence; and his determination to stand his ground, no matter the risks or the costs.

"I should have hit him," Jackson later said, "if he had shot me through the brain."

Over the coming years, other enemies would continue to test Jackson's tenacious resolve.

And every one of them, from battlefield adversaries to political opponents, would regret it.

"The Preservation and Success of the Republican Principle Rest with Us"

By the time Andrew Jackson arrived in the White House twenty-three years later, he was more than a president. He was an icon. In 1815 he had accomplished what had eluded even the beloved George Washington when Jackson brought the British army to its knees without the help of a strong foreign ally. In 1824 he had become a kind of political martyr when he won the popular vote for the presidency but lost the White House after one of his opponents allied with another opponent, allegedly in exchange for being named secretary of state.

In 1828 he avenged himself at the ballot box with a landslide victory produced by a swell of support from a nation that considered the rough-around-the-edges son of immigrants the first People's President—not only *for* the people but *of* the people.

In Jackson's first term, one of the great domestic battles concerned Senator Henry Clay's plan for expansive (and expensive) internal improvements—roads, bridges, and infrastructure projects that Clay believed would spur economic progress and territorial expansion.

The nationalist in Jackson liked the idea of growing the economy and strengthening the nation. He was fiercely prounion and utterly rejected the notion of a loose confederation of independent states. When South Carolina had threatened to nullify a federal law or secede from the union, Jackson had defiantly told a South Carolinian, "Please give my compliments to my friends in your state, and say to them that if a single drop of blood shall be shed there in opposition to the laws of the United States, I will hang the first man I can lay my hands on, engaged in such treasonable conduct, upon the first tree I can reach."[2]

Nevertheless, despite his belief in a strong union and his unequivocal vow to enforce federal laws, Jackson did not believe the Constitution gave the federal government the power to do something simply because its goal was good. True, some good policy could be advanced by Congress. But other good policy could be advanced only by the states. There were some things—even some *good* things—that Congress could not do. "The Federal Constitution must be obeyed," he told his confidant and secretary of state, Martin Van Buren. "State rights," he said, "must be preserved."

Jackson's belief that the Constitution placed significant limits on Congress—limits beyond those spelled out in the Bill of Rights—was far from novel. During his lifetime, the belief was nearly universal. After all, in Article I, the Constitution *listed* the powers of Congress; it made little sense to *list* certain powers if Congress actually had *all* powers. And as if that simple and seemingly obvious deduction were not clear enough, the Tenth Amendment had made this foundational principle explicit: "The powers not delegated to the United States by the Constitution, nor prohibited by it to the States, are reserved to the States respectively, or to the people."

The debate in Jackson's time was not over whether Congress's powers had limits; it was over the *precise contours* of those limits. Could Congress make regulations that had traditionally been made by the states? Could Congress pass laws addressing conduct that affected only the people inside a single state? Could Congress spend money on projects that existed within only one state?

On this last question Clay was sure the answer was a resounding "yes," and in 1830 Congress passed a law appropriating funds for a sixty-mile road within Clay's home state of Kentucky, stretching from Maysville to Lexington. Clay believed this kind of highway was crucial to connecting farms and factories and would make the United States a stronger, more prosperous, and more cohesive nation.

The Maysville road seemed to some like a small matter, but Jackson saw a larger principle at stake. In addition to its cost, its infringement on the prerogative of states bothered the president. If a road began and ended in one state, it seemed like a real stretch to characterize it as a national matter. And if it was not a national matter, it was not a matter for the federal government.

For Jackson this was not merely a theoretical question. Liberty was at stake. As the founding generation understood so well, in America there is an undeniable link among liberty, limits on federal power, and the preservation of states' prerogatives. In Jackson's words, the "consolidation and destruction of state rights" would be "destructive to the . . . liberty of the people." If the federal government could "wield its power in . . . the interior concerns of the state, this would lead to consolidation and that would destroy the liberty of your country."[3]

Thus, when Jackson learned that Congress had passed the Maysville Road Bill, he was skeptical. His instinct was to veto it. He began working on a veto message to Congress. But on the day the final decision was to be made, he met in the early morning over breakfast with his closest advisers to give them one last chance to persuade him not to veto the law.

Over breakfast, Jackson could see fear on the faces of some of his advisers. They dreaded the effect of a veto on Jackson's political capital in western states like Kentucky. They agreed with a congressman who had warned Jackson that if he vetoed the bill, Clay would destroy Jackson's political allies in the West like a hammer pounding on an anvil: "If this hand were an anvil on which the sledge hammer of the smith was descending and a fly were to light upon it in time to receive the blow, he would not crush it more effectually than you will crush your friends in Kentucky if you veto that Bill!"[4]

Later that day, when Van Buren mentioned the fear on the faces of Jackson's advisers at breakfast, Jackson said, "Yes, but don't mind that!" Then, pointing to the veto message written on the sheet of paper in his coat pocket, the president told Van Buren, "The thing is here, and shall be sent up as soon as Congress convenes."

Van Buren should not have been surprised by Jackson's political courage. This was, after all, the man whose physical courage had allowed him to face off with the best shooter in Tennessee and stand like a wall in the line of Charles Dickinson's bullet. Given that Jackson had refused to back down when faced with Charles Dickinson, there should have been little doubt that he would refuse to back down to Henry Clay.

Nevertheless, when Jackson's veto message arrived in Congress, it struck like a bolt of lightning—electrifying those who agreed with his vision of the Constitution and inflaming those who supported Clay's vision of federally funded internal improvements.

The message began with an explanation of the constitutional principle Jackson believed he was duty bound to apply: Appropriations should be limited to matters "of a general, not local" character; a "national, not State" nature. "A disregard of this distinction would of necessity lead to the subversion of the federal system."

Jackson then moved quickly to an application of this principle to the bill before him. "I have given to its provisions," he told Congress, "all the reflection demanded by a just regard for the interests of those of our fellow-citizens who have desired its passage, and by the respect which is due to a coordinate branch of the Government, but I am not able to view it in any other light than as a measure of purely local character." The Maysville road "has no connection with any established system of improvements," and it "is exclusively within the limits of a State."

Jackson did not question whether road construction was a good policy, but he knew that sometimes good policies must be enacted by states, not the federal government. It is a principle of republican government—one of great prominence and special importance in our constitutional system—that an unconstitutional law cannot be deemed constitutional simply because it promotes sound, laudable policies. Jackson wrote, "The preservation and success of the republican principle rest with us."

Toward the end of his message, Jackson addressed those who had so little faith in the American people that they believed the nation's citizens would be angry with Congress and the president if they declined to enact a law that, while designed with the noblest of objectives in mind, was ultimately unconstitutional. "If . . . the people of this country, reckless of their constitutional obligations, will prefer their local interest to the principles of the Union," then the world has "little to hope from the example of free government."

Although not as eloquent as Lincoln, Jackson tried to capture the notion Lincoln would later articulate when he said the American experiment was a test of whether not only *this* nation, but "*any* nation," if founded on our republican principles, "can long endure." Jackson proclaimed, "When an honest observance of constitutional compacts cannot be obtained from communities like ours, it need not be anticipated elsewhere." In that sad scenario, the people would have no "shield" against "the insidious advances" of ever-expanding federal power, and we would have to admit "the degrading truth that man is unfit for self-government." That "will be the case if expediency be made a rule of construction in interpreting the Constitution."[5]

After Jackson's veto, Henry Clay predicted that Jackson would pay a high political price. But Jackson had more confidence in the American people. "Where it has lost me one, it has gained me five friends," said the president. "The great body of the people hail the [veto], as a preservative of the constitution and the union." He told Van Buren that they had "nothing to fear from it."

Jackson did not stop with his veto of the Maysville Road Bill. Shortly afterward he vetoed the Washington Turnpike Bill. Then "he annulled the appropriations for building lighthouses and beacons, dredging harbors, and other such improvements. He also killed a bill to purchase stock in the Louisville and Portland Canal Company."[6] In the words of a Jackson biographer, "It was quite a massacre. But Jackson glowed."[7]

The Courage of Andrew Jackson

Jackson not only survived his veto of the Maysville Road Bill; he thrived. Despite his veto—or perhaps in part because of it—Jackson crushed Henry Clay in the reelection campaign of 1832, with Jackson taking 219 of 275 electoral votes. With the exception of Clay's home state, the entire West—the region that Jackson's advisers had worried would abandon him after the Maysville veto—threw its electoral votes behind Jackson.

By the time Andrew Jackson left office in 1837, he was the most popular president since George Washington, and it's possible that no other president since Jackson has left office more beloved by such a large percentage of the people. As one of his early biographers explained, "Columbus had sailed; Raleigh and the Puritans had planted; Franklin had lived; Washington fought; Jefferson written; fifty years of democratic government had passed; free schools, a free press, a voluntary church had done what they could to instruct the people; the population of the country had been quadrupled and its resources increased ten fold; and the result of all was, that the people of the United States had arrived at the capacity of honoring Andrew Jackson before all other living men."[8]

Such was the hold Jackson enjoyed over the hearts of his countrymen that in 1860, fifteen years after he died, some Americans were still voting for him for president, convinced that only his ghost could save America from the fast-approaching Civil War.[9]

While many today would understandably regard Jackson's vision of federal authority as far too narrow, our nation would be far better served if more leaders understood, as Jackson did, that the federal government's powers have limits. Even if he drew the line between federal power and state power more narrowly than even the most conservative members of Congress today, at least he was willing to draw it! Too many in Washington today refuse even to *recognize that a line exists*, let alone enforce it. Those politicians could learn a lot from Jackson's courage to act on his own carefully considered convictions. Just as Jackson did what he believed was right in 1806 when he defended his honor and calmly faced down the best shot in all of Tennessee, Jackson did what he believed was right in 1830 when he calmly faced down Henry Clay and defended the Constitution's limits.

Franklin Roosevelt Versus the Supreme Court

One hundred years after Andrew Jackson left office, on the evening of March 9, 1937, Americans turned on their radios to hear the familiar accent and distinctive, powerful cadence of a very different president. As usual, his voice was full of vigor and youthful vitality. Very few Americans had any idea that he was speaking to them from a wheelchair.

"Tonight, sitting at my desk in the White House," said Franklin Delano Roosevelt, "I make my first radio report to the people in my second term of office."

By 1937 Roosevelt's fireside chats were eagerly anticipated by Americans living through an uncertain era. Four years earlier, in his first radio address, he had explained the complicated banking crisis in terms every American could understand. In a matter of minutes, he had almost single-handedly restored the confidence of millions of citizens, especially those who had been making runs on banks that were closing by the thousands.

Roosevelt had become the father figure of the nation—a dominant, reassuring force in most Americans' everyday lives. In November 1936 he had won the largest landslide in the history of the United States with 61 percent of the popular vote and nearly every single vote in the Electoral College. His New Deal coalition—propelled by progressives, women, racial minorities, and labor unions—was a powerful force, one that he believed gave him an unusually strong mandate to pursue his unusually aggressive agenda.[10]

With the Republicans in Congress vastly outnumbered and on their heels, the only potential remaining check on FDR's power was the United States Supreme Court, which had served as that check in his first term. In 1935 it struck down a law creating pensions for railroad workers. That same year it struck down a law providing subsidies for and imposing regulations on America's farms. In 1936 it struck down a law regulating coal companies. In every case the Court held that Congress had exceeded its enumerated powers.

The most significant challenge to the New Deal arose when a small, family-run company that slaughtered and sold chickens in an entirely local market challenged the constitutionality of regulations imposed on it by the National Industrial Recovery Act. The regulatory agency created by the act—known as the National Recovery Administration—was empowered to regulate vast swaths of economic life in America by setting minimum wages, fixing prices, regulating trade, and establishing maximum hours for workers. The agency even had its own mascot—the Blue Eagle. Paying a disturbing, un-American kind of homage to this new, powerful, government agency, shopkeepers displayed the Blue Eagle in their store windows to advertise their compliance with the regulatory rules, and chorus girls wore emblems of the bird on their costumes.[11] Consumers, meanwhile, were encouraged to shop only where the Blue Eagle was proudly displayed. In fact, the mascot inspired the name of the NFL franchise created in Philadelphia in 1933, the Philadelphia Eagles.

Fortunately for the Constitution, the Blue Eagle proved no match for the Supreme Court. The Court invalidated the legislation creating the National Recovery Administration, declaring it unconstitutional because neither the commerce clause nor any other provision of the Constitution authorizes Congress to regulate local commerce.

The commerce clause gives Congress the power "to regulate Commerce with foreign Nations, and among the several States, and with the Indian Tribes." By implication, Congress's limited powers do not extend to the regulation of commerce that is *not* "with foreign Nations" or "among the several States" or "with the Indian Tribes." The Tenth Amendment confirms that those limits exist and that powers beyond those limits belong to the states.

By the mid-1930s, the commerce clause had long been understood to authorize Congress to regulate not only interstate and international commercial transactions but also channels and instrumentalities of interstate and international commerce (for example, interstate highways, waterways, airways, etc.). But neither the founding generation nor the majority of Supreme Court justices from the time of Chief Justice John Marshall to the dawn of the New Deal regarded economic activity occurring entirely within one state as interstate commerce, even though the economic activity in one state might *affect* commerce in other states. Thus, for the first century and a half of American history, intrastate economic activities like labor, manufacturing, agriculture, and mining were not considered appropriate subjects for federal legislation under the commerce clause. Congress had rarely attempted to regulate in these areas, and when it did so the legislation encountered difficulties in court.

Roosevelt's New Deal programs relied on a revolutionary interpretation of the commerce clause. His theory suggested all transactions had an *effect* on interstate commerce and could therefore be regulated. It was this theory that the Court repeatedly rejected in Roosevelt's first term because "the authority of the federal government may not be pushed to such an extreme as to destroy the distinction, which the commerce clause itself establishes, between commerce 'among the several States' and the internal concerns of a State."[12]

So, in this fireside chat on March 9, 1937, the president set his sights on the Court.

By striking down parts of the New Deal, FDR charged, Roosevelt alleged that the Court "improperly set itself up as a third house of the Congress."[13] He claimed we had "reached the point as a nation where we must take action to save the Constitution from the Court and the Court from itself. We must find a way to take an appeal from the Supreme Court to the Constitution itself."

Speaking into a radio microphone in a largely empty room, the president compared "the American form of government" to "a three horse team provided by the Constitution to the American people so that their field might be plowed." The patrician Roosevelt hardly had much experience plowing actual fields, but he was always searching for clever metaphors to illustrate abstract principles. "The three horses are, of course, the three branches of government—the Congress, the Executive, and the Courts."

With regret, Roosevelt informed the public that only "two of the horses are pulling in unison today." The stubborn third horse was, he asserted, defying the will of the American people. "It is the American people themselves who are in the driver's seat," said Roosevelt, extending the metaphor. "It is the American people themselves who want the furrow plowed. It is the American people themselves who expect the third horse to pull in unison with the other two."

"What is my proposal?" asked Roosevelt. "It is simply this: Whenever a judge or justice of any federal court has reached the age of seventy and does not avail himself of the opportunity to retire on a pension, a new member shall be appointed by the president then in office." It just so happened that there were five jurists serving on the Supreme Court who were at that moment older than seventy. Accordingly, Roosevelt was proposing the creation of *five new positions* on the Supreme Court. With that addition of "younger men who have had personal experience and contact with modern facts and circumstances under which average men have to live and work," FDR would go from losing cases by a vote of five to four to winning them by a vote of nine to five. "This plan," the president promised, would "save our national Constitution from hardening of the judicial arteries."

In the previous four years, Americans tuning in to Roosevelt's fireside chats had heard some radical ideas for economic reform and regulation. But never before had the president proposed anything as audacious as an "appeal" from the decisions of the Supreme Court, which had been resolving disputes involving the constitutionality of federal laws since Chief Justice John Marshall authored the Court's 1803 decision in *Marbury v. Madison*. Marshall had insisted, "It is emphatically the province of the Judicial Department to say what the law is" and to invalidate unconstitutional laws properly challenged in court.[14]

To those who would call this a plan for "packing the Court," the president promised to "answer this question with a bluntness that will end all honest misunderstanding of my purposes." He would not appoint "spineless puppets." But if "packing the Court" meant appointing men who understand the "modern conditions" of social and economic life—and not men "fearful of the future"—then "I say that I and with me the vast majority of the American people favor doing just that thing—now."

Roosevelt may well have been correct when he predicted that the "vast majority of the American people" would support his plan. We will never know. It took just over two months before, in the face of Roosevelt's threat to pack the Court and fundamentally alter the balance of power between the judicial and political branches, the Supreme Court retreated.

"The Switch in Time That Saved Nine"

The retreat became official on the morning of April 12, 1937, in the marbled courtroom of the Supreme Court.[15]

In the case before the Court, *National Labor Relations Board v. Jones & Laughlin Steel*, the justices were asked to uphold the constitutionality of the National Labor Relations Act, which was similar to the law regulating coal companies that the Court had struck down only the previous year. Both statutes regulated the relationship between management and labor in businesses engaged in local commerce. In both cases Roosevelt's lawyers had argued that the commerce being regulated was "interstate" because local businesses were part of a national industry, and even if they did not participate in interstate commerce, they *had an effect on* interstate commerce.

Five votes were needed to uphold the New Deal law, but when the case was argued in February, only four justices (at best) were expected to be on board. That assumption changed when the Court was gaveled into session on April 12 and Chief Justice Hughes declared that *he* would be announcing the decision of the Court. Astute observers in the courtroom understood what that meant—that Hughes, a reliable vote for Roosevelt's New Deal, was in the majority.

Despite his appointment by two Republican presidents—first (as associate justice) by President William Howard Taft, and later (as chief justice) by President Herbert Hoover—Hughes was not a reliable conservative on the Court. The son of a minister, known for his generous facial hair and whimsical eyebrows, Hughes had proved a fairly dependable vote for Roosevelt's New Deal programs. For four years the chief justice had often found himself in the minority in a Court dominated by conservatives skeptical of federal power. But not today. Today everything was changing.

Although the chief justice authored and announced the ruling, his was not the vote that mattered. Everyone knew that one of the conservative justices had switched sides and joined the bloc of justices sympathetic to the FDR administration's expansive reading of the commerce clause.

That jurist was Associate Justice Owen Roberts. Appointed by President Hoover, Roberts had made his name fighting corruption in the Teapot Dome Scandal as an assistant district attorney in Philadelphia.

On this day Roberts sat impassively as the decision was read beneath stately marble friezes depicting famous lawgivers like Hammurabi and Moses. Speculation immediately surfaced that Roberts had switched his vote in order to avoid the constitutional crisis Roosevelt had precipitated when he announced his Court-packing scheme.

Roberts's vote in *Jones & Laughlin* and in a host of cases that followed—known forever afterward as "the switch in time that saved nine"—guaranteed that Roosevelt would never deliver the Court's death blow. There was no need for it now; Roberts had eliminated Roosevelt's reason for wanting to pack the Court.

Whatever his reasons—he did not share them—Roberts had been the linchpin in a stunning act of reversal for the Court. In order to reach that outcome, the Court retreated from the founding-era understanding that the Congress's commerce-clause authority has meaningful limits and that those limits must be enforced by the courts. In doing so, the Court largely nullified the Tenth Amendment's declaration that "powers not delegated to the United States by the Constitution"—like the power to regulate *intra*state commerce—"are reserved to the States respectively, or to the people." The Court now reasoned that certain "intrastate activities [that had previously been deemed beyond Congress's power to regulate], by reason of close and intimate relation to interstate commerce, may fall within federal control."[16]

During the seventy-five years following the "switch in time that saved nine," Congress passed laws regulating almost every aspect of economic life in America, no matter how local in nature the commerce. It even authorized limits on the amount of wheat a farmer can grow to feed his own livestock. It also passed a host of *noneconomic* regulations with only the most tenuous relation to any kind of commerce, be it *inter*state or *intra*state. In all that time, from April 12, 1937, through June 27, 2012, the Court invalidated only two laws as beyond Congress's commerce-clause power, and neither of the two laws (part of a gun-control law and part of a law addressing violence against women) was even an economic regulation.

There was every reason to believe that in the wake of President Roosevelt's manipulation of the Supreme Court, the federal government, under the commerce clause, had the power to do *anything*.

All Eyes on Kennedy

The Supreme Court had a chance to correct that error in 2012, when it considered the constitutionality of Obamacare's individual mandate. The mandate required essentially every American to purchase health insurance and imposed penalties on those who failed to comply. Its opponents believed that even if Congress could regulate almost any *activity*, it lacked the authority to regulate *inactivity*—i.e., the decision by an American citizen to *not* purchase insurance. In other words, regardless of the limits on Congress's power to *regulate* commerce, there was no constitutional authority to *compel* commerce.

On March 27, 2012, the Court heard oral arguments about whether the commerce clause empowered Congress to force Americans to purchase health insurance. As usual, many eyes in the marble courtroom were closely watching Justice Anthony Kennedy, often the decisive vote on the Court, for any sign of how he might lean in the case.

Several minutes after the argument began, Justice Kennedy tipped his hand in a not-so-subtle way. "Assume for the moment," he told the solicitor general (who was defending the individual mandate), "that this is unprecedented. This is a step beyond what our cases have allowed, the affirmative duty to act to go into commerce. If that is so, do you not have a heavy burden of justification?"[17] Of course, the solicitor general had argued vigorously in his written brief that the individual mandate was not unprecedented. Justice Kennedy's question was not a good omen for him.

As the argument continued, Kennedy kept criticizing the legitimacy of the mandate. "Here the government is saying that the federal government has a duty to tell the individual citizen that it must act," explained Kennedy, "and that is different from what we have in previous cases. And that changes the relationship of the federal government to the individual in a very fundamental way."

When Kennedy asserted without qualification that Obamacare's individual mandate fundamentally alters the relationship between the government and the governed, observers could see the looks of fear and shock on the faces of liberals throughout the courtroom. They were doomed if Justice Kennedy understood that a federal government empowered to make you buy health insurance is empowered to make you do *anything*.

Justice Alito made this point clear when he asked the solicitor general, "Could you express your limiting principle as succinctly as you can?" In other words, could the solicitor general succinctly explain what, if anything, Congress *cannot* do if Congress can pass the individual mandate?

The solicitor general, Donald B. Verrilli Jr., is a smart lawyer and a hard worker. He had undoubtedly prepared for hours upon hours in anticipation of the argument that would help define his career as an appellate advocate. It is a virtual certainty that he spent a substantial amount of time preparing just for this question, which was sure to be asked and sure to be crucial to the Court's decision.

And yet he had no answer—at least no succinct answer that identified an actual "limiting principle" to the Obama administration's interpretation of the commerce clause. That was not because of a lack of skill or preparation. It was because there *was* no answer. Proponents of the individual mandate had no limiting principle. They believed Congress *could* pass any law, directed at anyone, related to any topic, regardless of whether the regulated issue was interstate, regardless of whether it was commercial, and regardless of whether it concerned activity or inactivity. Their philosophy was "I am, therefore I can be regulated."

By the close of the next day, after seven and a half hours of argument, it appeared to legal commentators in the courtroom that a majority of the justices had not been fooled by the Obama administration's attempt to portray the individual mandate as a regulation of interstate commerce. Among that apparent majority was Justice Kennedy, the judicial conservative whom analysts considered most likely to side with the four liberals on the Court.

But Court watchers were looking at the wrong justice.

Another Roberts, Another Surrender

Three months and a day after the oral arguments on Obamacare, in a hushed courtroom full of lawyers, reporters, and concerned citizens hanging on his every word, Chief Justice John Roberts began his announcement of the Court's decision. Many of the observers sitting in the courtroom believed that since the conservative Roberts was announcing the Court's ruling, the justices had overturned Obamacare. Conservatives felt elated at the prospect. Liberals sat stone-faced, trying to hide their disappointment.

And yet, just as *Owen* Roberts had saved President Roosevelt's New Deal, *John* Roberts found a way to save Obamacare's individual mandate. He slowly and calmly announced that, although the commerce clause did not give Congress the power to make Americans buy health insurance, the taxation clause *did* give Congress the authority it needed.

Every American knows the federal government has the power to impose taxes. According to Chief Justice John Roberts, the penalty for not buying insurance is just another tax. All it took was a little sleight of hand. Roberts needed only to delete Obamacare's command that Americans "shall" buy insurance; replace the command with a mere encouragement to buy insurance; and call the mandate's "penalty" for not buying insurance a "tax."

Consequently, a decision that initially appeared to limit Congress's regulatory power turned out to be something closer to an expansion of that power. Under the Court's new rule, Congress can pass any regulation it wants, and the Court will uphold it by calling the penalty for violating that regulation a "tax." I explain this and other aspects of the ruling in my 2013 e-book, *Why John Roberts Was Wrong About Healthcare: A Conservative Critique of the Supreme Court's Obamacare Ruling.*

As Justice Kennedy explained from the bench on behalf of the four dissenting justices (the other dissenters were Justice Scalia, Justice Thomas, and Justice Alito), the decision of the Court was a blow to the structure of the Constitution—a structure that matters as much today as it did in 1787. "There are structural limits upon Congress's powers," said Kennedy. "In other words, there are some things the Federal Government cannot do." There may be some people who think the freedom of Americans is more affected by cases about individuals rights, like the freedom of speech or equal protection under the law, than by cases about federalism, separation of powers, and other elements of the Constitution's structure. "But structure means liberty." That is because "without structure, there are insufficient means to hold to account a central government that exceeds its powers in controlling the lives of its citizens."

The Supreme Court, said Justice Kennedy, could have vindicated this principle.

Instead, the majority of the Court ignored it.

PART II

Reclaiming the Lost Clauses

CHAPTER 7

Reclaiming the Constitution Through the Courts

In 1803 AN OBSCURE OFFICE SEEKER ASKED THE UNITED STATES Supreme Court to order the secretary of state to make him a justice of the peace. He relied in part on an act of Congress called the Judiciary Act, which established the federal court system. Under the terms of the statute, the office seeker was entitled to the court order he sought. But the Supreme Court ruled against him, holding that Congress lacked the authority to pass part of the Judiciary Act. The office seeker was William Marbury. The case was *Marbury v. Madison*.

In his opinion, Chief Justice John Marshall explained why the Court has the authority to invalidate a statute that a legislature lacks the authority to enact. The Constitution is "the fundamental and paramount law of the nation."[1] Consequently, "an act of the Legislature repugnant to the Constitution is void." Judges must not allow those "void" statutes to govern the cases before the courts, because doing so "would subvert the very foundation of all written Constitutions" by allowing a legislature to "do what is expressly forbidden."

Of course, judges are not the only government officials with a duty to interpret the Constitution and to abide by its rules. Like judges, legislators and presidents swear to defend the Constitution, and as subsequent chapters suggest, voters should demand that they adhere to their oath. It is a mistake to expect courts to single-handedly revive the Lost Constitution.

Nevertheless, there is a role for courts to play. As Marshall famously wrote in *Marbury*, "It is emphatically the province and duty of the Judicial Department to say what the law is." When judges perform that duty by refusing to give effect to an unconstitutional law, they preserve the "distinction between a government with limited and unlimited powers."

While subsequent chapters of this book look at the opportunities and responsibilities for legislators and voters in the effort to revive the Lost Constitution, this chapter considers the role of courts. And there is no better example of the positive impact courts can make in resurrecting the Lost Constitution than the recent history of litigation over the Second Amendment.

For many years the Second Amendment was part of the Lost Constitution. The U.S. Supreme Court gave little attention to the Constitution's command that "the right of the people to keep and bear arms shall not be infringed." In fact, to say the Second Amendment received little attention may be an understatement. The Court alternated between ignoring it and undercutting it. This, of course, was a bizarre departure from the explicit intentions of America's founders.

What follows is the story of the rationale of the Second Amendment—which began even before we declared our independence—and the history of how a vital clause in the Lost Constitution was recently resurrected by unyielding litigants and a conservative majority on the Supreme Court. It is a tale of kings and bank robbers; revolutions and constitutions; and a small band of liberty-loving Americans who just a few years ago believed they could accomplish the impossible.

Taking His Countrymen's Guns Away

In 1671 King Charles II had a problem. His father had been beheaded by political enemies. In the period following that regicide, the royal family's rival, Oliver Cromwell, had led an army of sixty thousand troops,[2] and although the monarchy had returned to power after Cromwell died of malaria, the former soldiers of Cromwell's disbanded army still distrusted the crown. And they still had their guns.

Not wishing to share his father's fate, Charles II wanted nothing more than to disarm his political opponents.[3] But he knew that his subjects considered gun ownership a God-given right. Philosophers and statesmen from Aristotle to Cicero had recognized a natural right to carry weapons in defense of one's life and home. In the seventeenth century Englishmen used guns both to hunt for the food that fed their families and to defend against the bandits who threatened their wives and children. In a nation without standing police forces, life without a weapon was a frightening prospect.

Nevertheless, Charles II decided to take his countrymen's guns away. He began with disarmaments targeted at political opponents, but in 1671 Parliament decided to go even further. Under the guise of regulating hunting, but principally motivated by a desire to disarm political opponents, Parliament passed the Game Act.[4] The new law declared that commoners were "not allowed to have or keepe for themselves or any other person or persons any Guns, Bowes, Grey hounds, Setting-dogs, Ferretts, Cony-doggs, Lurchers, Hayes, Netts, Lowbells, Hare-pipes, Ginns, Snares or other Engines aforesaid."[5] In other words, if you were a commoner, you were losing your gun—and your dog!

England's Bill of Rights

Fast-forward seventeen years. The reign of James II, son of the deceased Charles II, had thus far been a rocky one. After attempting to impose his Catholicism on a largely Protestant country, James had faced rebellions in the south and in the north. The king's men had easily quelled each revolt, but James could never be sure when the next revolution would arise. In a combination of zeal and paranoia, he began to abuse a little-noticed provision of the Game Act. It allowed for searches of homes to confiscate the many weapons that families had kept hidden away in defiance of the law.

Before long, the king's searches began, and countless Protestants soon enjoyed little security or privacy within the walls of their homes. Doors were broken down. Strangers with warrants ransacked rooms. Wives and daughters were undoubtedly assaulted. And entire families were left unable to hunt for food or protect themselves against crime.

By 1688 the English had had enough. They invited James's daughter Mary and her Dutch husband William to depose James and restore liberty to their island. In the Glorious Revolution, William and Mary did exactly that. After landing in Britain unopposed, they accepted the terms of a new legal instrument—a bill of rights. Among its other guarantees, it promised "that the subjects which are Protestants may have arms for their defense suitable to their conditions and as allowed by law."

The English Bill of Rights codified what the legendary English legal authority William Blackstone would call a fundamental right: "the right of having and using arms for self-preservation and defence."[6]

"A Natural Right"

Over the next hundred years, the crown reigned over a period of relative tranquility in Britain. Never after William and Mary's Glorious Revolution was a British monarch deposed. But Britain was not yet free from dealing with revolutions. Across the ocean, its colonists were bristling at taxes compelled by an unrepresentative government, and beginning in the 1760s, those colonists started to demand the rights of Englishmen to which William and Mary had acceded.

In opposition to their demands, King George III decided to take a page out of the playbook of his gun-grabbing predecessors. Like the agents of Charles II and James II in the seventeenth century, King George III's redcoats broke down doors in American homes and searched for weapons. Colonists lost the feeling of security and the guarantee of privacy that their homes had once afforded them. At the same time, as occupying armies and Crown-controlled governors took power from locally elected assemblies, the colonists began to feel that their destinies were in the hands of a distant and domineering despot.

Editorials in colonial newspapers vented the outrage of the English colonists who believed that the English Bill of Rights protected them against such abuses. It is "a natural right," declared a typical editorial in New York, "which the people have reserved to themselves, confirmed by the Bill of Rights, to keep arms for their own defence."[7]

Editorials and unrest led to revolution, and after the United States secured its independence at Yorktown, it was never uncertain whether Americans would create a government that secured the right of self-government and the civil liberties guaranteed in the English Bill of Rights. Following the ineffectiveness of the Articles of Confederation, the American people ratified a Constitution proclaiming that "We the People" would rule. And it was widely presumed that those "People" were not only entitled to but depended on their guns. As Alexander Hamilton had written in the *Federalist Papers*, the "original right of self-defense . . . is paramount to all positive forms of government."[8]

Because of the paramount importance of that right, when the United States ratified the Bill of Rights in 1791, near the top of the list of freedoms protected was the Second Amendment: "A well regulated Militia, being necessary to the security of a free State, the right of the people to keep and bear Arms, shall not be infringed."

The founding generation expected the Second Amendment to endure and protect gun owners for centuries.

Unfortunately, it didn't.

Judge Hiram Ragon's Trick

The road east from Jackson "Jack" Miller's home in Claremont, Oklahoma, was not in the best of conditions. Few rural roads were. But the views as Miller's car climbed up into the Ozarks on April 18, 1938, were nothing to complain about.[9]

With his friend Frank Layton, Jack Miller—who had once killed a man with a punch to the jaw and had driven the getaway car for one of the era's most successful gangs of bank robbers—had driven about seventy miles that day.[10] With the two men in the car was a sawed-off shotgun. This was a business trip, and their business was crime.

It wasn't long after Miller and Layton crossed the border into Arkansas that Miller's heart sank. Perhaps tipped off by one of Miller's enemies, state police from Arkansas and Oklahoma were there, pulling them over and, before long, searching their car. As soon as the police found the shotgun, Miller and Layton were under arrest.

In 1934 Congress had put a tax on certain unusual guns, including machine guns and sawed-off shotguns. An attempt to combat the rise of bootleggers and gangsters by controlling weapons, the tax was part of the National Firearms Act, an unprecedented federal attempt to target particularly dangerous weapons.[11] The tax functioned as a de facto ban in most instances because it was so high that hardly anyone could afford to pay it.

Jack Miller certainly couldn't—and hadn't.

Six weeks later, Miller and Layton were indicted in federal district court for taking the gun across state lines without paying the tax. Both tried to plead guilty. After all, tax evasion was hardly the worst crime they'd committed, and they figured they would be out of jail soon. But the district judge for the Western District of Arkansas, Hiram Ragon, had other plans for them.

Ragon was a New Deal Democrat. A congressman for ten years until President Franklin D. Roosevelt appointed him to the bench, Ragon had introduced federal gun-control legislation in the 1920s and had proclaimed himself "unequivocally opposed to pistols in any connection whatever."[12] Now, as a judge, he saw an opportunity to squelch opposition to the National Firearms Act and Roosevelt's gun-control agenda, both of which were viewed as important parts of a New Deal founded on the premise that the federal government can and should solve problems traditionally addressed by state and local officials.

The opposition to Roosevelt's gun-control efforts frequently cited the Second Amendment, and Ragon figured that the best way to combat that opposition would be to secure a Supreme Court ruling upholding the National Firearms Act's constitutionality. With that objective in mind, Ragon refused to accept Miller and Layton's guilty plea until they had an opportunity to consult with counsel. He then handpicked an attorney for them, and when the attorney argued that the National Firearms Act was unconstitutional, Ragon quickly agreed.

Judge Ragon's decision to dismiss the case included no argument or legal reasoning—and for good reason: Ragon didn't seem to believe his own ruling. A strong proponent of gun control, it appears likely he just wanted to tee up a clean case for the Supreme Court with two unsympathetic defendants, career criminals Jack Miller and Frank Layton.[13]

"We Cannot Say the Second Amendment Guarantees the Right to Bear Such an Instrument"

On March 30, 1939, Justice James Clark McReynolds looked across the courtroom as the Supreme Court was preparing to hear arguments in *United States v. Miller*. He was an aging, aristocratic curmudgeon with a deep southern accent and an abiding hatred for African Americans, Jews, and anyone who disagreed with him.

On this day McReynolds beheld an unusual scene. Normally, when a case is argued in front of the Supreme Court, opposing sets of lawyers appear, each presenting one side of the case. The lawyers for the petitioner or appellant (the party asking the Supreme Court to overturn the lower-court ruling) sit at one table, while those representing the respondent or appellee (the party defending the lower-court ruling) can be found seated at the other. But today was different. Attorney Gordon Dean was ready to represent the U.S. government, but no one was there to represent Jack Miller and Frank Layton.

After Judge Ragon had held the National Firearms Act unconstitutional, the government had asked the Supreme Court to overrule Ragon's decision. The justices had agreed to take the case and had asked the defendants' attorney, Paul Gutensohn, to file a brief and travel to Washington, D.C., for the oral arguments. Gutensohn, however, declined. Miller and Layton were long gone, having disappeared after being freed by Judge Ragon, and Gutensohn didn't think defending them on appeal was worth his time—or money. In a telegram referring to the government's brief, he told the Court: "Suggest case be submitted on Appellants brief. Unable to obtain any money from clients to be present and argue case = Paul E Gutensohn."[14]

At oral argument the government—without opposition— proposed two possible interpretations of the Second Amendment. First the government argued that the Second Amendment does not protect the rights of individuals and that its protections extend only to a collective right to bear arms in connection with the maintenance of an effective militia. Alternatively, the government argued that, even assuming the Second Amendment protects an individual right to bear arms, it could not be deemed to protect the types of guns at issue in the case at hand.

The government didn't particularly care which of these two interpretations the Supreme Court adopted. After all, under either interpretation, the government would be victorious. Did it really matter how the case was won?

When Justice McReynolds announced the Supreme Court's ruling in *United States v. Miller* six and a half weeks later, there were three losers. The first two were Miller and Layton. The third loser was the Second Amendment.

Significantly and to his credit, Justice McReynolds declined to interpret the Second Amendment to protect only militia members. Misanthrope or not, he was not inclined to disregard this provision of the Constitution in its entirety.

He was, however, more than willing to weaken it. Parts of his opinion ignored the Second Amendment altogether. Other parts reasoned that a sawed-off shotgun is not "any part of the ordinary military equipment" and would not "contribute to the common defense." Consequently, McReynolds hastily concluded, "we cannot say that the Second Amendment guarantees the right to keep and bear such an instrument" as the gun at issue.

The best reading of this opinion is that the Second Amendment does not protect the particular gun in the *Miller* case—a sawed-off shotgun. The implication of the opinion's focus on the gun is that Miller and Layton—and all of us!—have what the Second Amendment guarantees to us: an individual right to own certain other guns, including those that "contribute to the common defense."

Significant problems stemmed from the fact that this opinion was written in a lazy, sloppy, and at times incomprehensible fashion— unusual for an opinion issued by the Supreme Court of the United States, but less unusual for an opinion authored by Justice McReynolds. He filled around three quarters of the opinion in *Miller* with unwieldy lists of citations and interminably long quotations cut and pasted from other sources, rather than engaging in a thorough, original analysis.[15] Even more problematically, McReynolds failed to state explicitly what his opinion implied—that each of us has a right to possess ordinary weapons like regular shotguns, rifles, and pistols. His failure to be more explicit meant that enemies of the Second Amendment could read into the opinion whatever they wished.

And for the next sixty-nine years, that's exactly what they did. Not once in that time did the Supreme Court strike down a restriction on firearms based on the grounds that the regulation in question violated the Second Amendment of the Constitution.

"The Greatest Fraud on the American Public"

In 1991, five years after retiring from the bench, with his trademark mane of white hair thinned by age, former chief justice Warren Burger was asked about his opinion of the Second Amendment. This may at first have appeared to be an odd question. After all, Burger had served seventeen years on the Supreme Court. Wouldn't his decisions have made his opinion clear?

Warren Burger, however, had never once adjudicated a case with a holding that hinged on the Second Amendment. That's because the Supreme Court does not typically consider cases in which the lower courts are in agreement, and after *Miller*, no federal appellate court to consider the question concluded that the Second Amendment protected an individual citizen's right to possess a firearm.

This consensus manifested itself in many ways. In law schools, for example, constitutional law professors rarely made any mention of the Second Amendment. Students who spoke of this provision as if it remained applicable in modern society opened themselves up to ridicule. Academia's most famous constitutional law scholar, Harvard's Laurence Tribe, published a treatise on constitutional law in 1978 that literally relegated the Second Amendment to a footnote.[16]

Despite this consensus, Burger might have been expected to sympathize with gun-rights groups like the National Rifle Association. After all, he had once been actively involved in Republican politics. In 1969 President Nixon nominated him to the Supreme Court in an attempt to make the Court less liberal.

But Burger's response to the question about the Second Amendment made clear that he not only disagreed with gun-rights organizations; he had contempt for them. The Second Amendment, he said, "has been the subject of one of the greatest pieces of fraud, I repeat the word 'fraud,' on the American public by special interest groups that I have ever seen in my lifetime."[17] Presumably, the "special interest groups" he was referring to included the NRA and other like-minded organizations. The "fraud" Burger believed they had perpetrated was convincing the American people that the Second Amendment was relevant in the twentieth century.

The next year Burger followed up his "fraud" line with a speech declaring that "the Second Amendment doesn't guarantee the right to have firearms at all." The amendment's purpose, he claimed, was "to ensure that the 'state armies'—'the militia'—would be maintained for the defense of the state."[18]

In other words, if you weren't a member of a militia, you didn't have a Second Amendment right to anything. Not a pistol. Not a musket. Not even a pocket knife. This, in the 1990s, was the extent to which federal courts and elite lawyers had forgotten the Second Amendment's true meaning.

"We Ought to Challenge That"

Among the people who didn't agree with that conventional wisdom was Clark Neily. A determined advocate for libertarian causes, Neily was young, hard charging, well spoken, and passionate about defending the Constitution's protections of individual freedom. Although he was not exactly a firearms aficionado, he had grown up surrounded by hunters and understood enough about the Second Amendment to believe that law-abiding citizens have a constitutional right to keep and bear arms.[19]

In 2002 Neily and his colleague at the Institute for Justice, another young public-interest attorney named Steve Simpson, started talking to each other at a happy hour about the gun laws in their hometown, Washington, D.C. In 1976 the city council had passed a law prohibiting all usable firearms—even in the home. The capital city's laws were the most oppressive in the nation, and both attorneys agreed that *someone* really ought to challenge them in court.

Suddenly, according to Neily, there was "almost this comical moment, this brief pause when we both realize we're public interest lawyers, libertarian public interest lawyers who like guns, and one of us looks at the other and says, '*We* ought to challenge that.'"[20]

At a Georgetown social gathering, Neily and Simpson approached a man with considerable ability to make a protracted constitutional challenge possible. He had a bald head, enormous ears, and a pocketbook capable of funding a lawsuit that could last most of the decade. His name was Robert Levy.

Levy had made millions selling financial information and software in the 1980s. At age forty-nine he sold his company and then went to law school, clerked for a prestigious federal judge, and wound up chairman of the board of the Cato Institute, a prestigious libertarian think tank.

When Neily and Simpson met Levy at the Georgetown party, they made a compelling case for a lawsuit. The District of Columbia's law was clearly, in their view, unconstitutional. It appeared, moreover, to have done nothing to combat crime. Since the law's passage, D.C.'s murder rate had skyrocketed, and by 2003 it would be higher than Baghdad's.[21]

Equally important, the young lawyers convinced Levy that the timing was right. An increasing number of law-review articles had shown overwhelming evidence that the founding generation had understood the Second Amendment as guaranteeing Americans the right to protect themselves with guns. Moreover, in an unprecedented move by the Justice Department, Attorney General John Ashcroft had recently replied to a question from the NRA with a letter stating "unequivocally . . . that the text and the original intent of the Second Amendment clearly protect the right of individuals to keep and bear firearms," rather than guaranteeing "only a 'collective' right of the States to maintain militias."[22] And for the first time since *United States v. Miller*, a federal appellate court had recently broken with all other federal courts and concluded that the Second Amendment protects an *individual* right to bear arms.

Convinced of the lawsuit's merits and timing, Levy wasn't just willing to join Neily and Simpson in their crusade (which many dismissed as quixotic); he was willing to pay for every dollar it would cost to take a case from its inception all the way to the Supreme Court. Levy was determined to do everything he could to prove that interpreting the Second Amendment to protect Americans' firearms was, contrary to Warren Burger's dismissive epithets, far from a "fraud."

Now all they needed was a client.

They found one in a sixty-year-old, gray-haired army veteran. His name was Dick Heller.

"Denied"

When Dick Heller arrived at the police station on July 17, 2002, he had a simple request. He wanted the District of Columbia to register a handgun he had bought legally before the city's gun laws were enacted in 1976.[23]

Heller had good reasons for his request. He lived in a high-crime neighborhood in northeast D.C. Drug dealers had seized control of a housing project near his home. Random shootings were common. A bullet had found its way to his front door. Another had flown through his window. Men had broken down his neighbor's door, put a gun to her head, and robbed her in a "kick and enter" robbery that had become all too common in the neighborhood. For a time, a drug dealer across the street fired a gun every night at precisely 2:00 a.m. to signal—like a school bell or a factory buzzer—the end of the workday.

Not only did Heller have good reasons for wanting a gun in his home; he was the epitome of a responsible would-be gun owner. By day, Heller was a licensed special police officer who worked at the Federal Judicial Center. While protecting federal employees and federal judges during the day, he was trusted with—and required to carry—a pistol. But while the local laws in Washington *required* Heller to keep that gun at work, they *prohibited* him from keeping a gun at home, even though he lived in a neighborhood overrun with violent criminals.

Heller didn't expect the city to register his gun. It would have been contrary to local gun-control laws had the city done so. But he had by then joined forces with Richard Levy after being introduced to the millionaire through a mutual acquaintance, and he wanted to be able to show a court that he had at least tried to exercise his Second Amendment rights.

When Heller walked out of the police station, he left with an application stamped with a single word: "Denied."

"There Is a Right to Bear Arms"

The path from filing a complaint in a trial court to litigating in an appellate court is not for the faint of heart or for the impatient. The process is mind-bogglingly expensive. And even once you've made it to the stage when you can ask the Supreme Court to hear your case, your chances of the Court's agreeing to take it stand at less than 1 percent. But six long years after Dick Heller had been denied his gun permit, the Supreme Court was ready to hear his argument.

Heller's case had not had a glamorous start; the District of Columbia's litigation office forgot about it. The suit and with it the notion that the Second Amendment protects an individual right to a firearm in the twenty-first century—was considered so preposterous that the city didn't remember to file a response to challenge it. Only after the court granted the city an extension of the deadline for a response did the city bother to fight Heller's suit. Apparently it never occurred to anyone working for the city that any judge in the city might actually agree with Dick Heller.

Heller, however, defied the odds. Not only did he win before the U.S. Court of Appeals for the D.C. Circuit, but he made it all the way to the Supreme Court. So, on a Tuesday morning in March 2008, less than a mile from the police station where Heller's application for a firearm registration had been denied, it was with great satisfaction that Heller heard the clerk of court announce the familiar incantation, "Oyez! Oyez! Oyez! All persons having business before the Honorable, the Supreme Court of the United States, are admonished to draw near and give their attention, for the Court is now sitting. God save the United States and this Honorable Court." With that, the Clerk gaveled into session the case of *District of Columbia v. Heller*. Mr. Heller had business before the Court that day—business that would have ramifications for some 300 million Americans.

Between the courtroom's massive columns and within its white marbled walls, the audience of attorneys, reporters, and other spectators sat with rapt attention as justices fired questions at the attorneys. Many of those who knew the Court well suspected the four liberal justices would never support Heller, so when the Court's swing justice, Anthony Kennedy, first spoke—just a few minutes after the argument began—Heller and his team held their breath. Without Justice Kennedy's vote, it would be almost impossible to win.

"The amendment," said Kennedy in the midst of a long question, "says we reaffirm the right to have a militia. We've established it."

If Kennedy had stopped there, it would have been bad news for Heller. If the Second Amendment protected only a militia, Heller—and all individual gun owners in modern times—would remain unprotected by it.

"But," continued Kennedy, to Heller's enormous relief, "in addition, there is a right to bear arms. Can you comment on that?"

The question was aimed at the city's attorney, but no one in the room believed Kennedy was really asking a question. He was opining, and it appeared he was inclined to believe the Second Amendment protects *more* than militias. The amendment, "in addition," protects the right of people like Heller to own a gun.

It was an "electric moment" for Clark Neily, the young lawyer who, with his friend Steve Simpson, had first persuaded Levy to launch the case that was now before the Supreme Court. He knew after Kennedy's question that the Court's swing justice was probably on their side. And he knew that if they had won over Kennedy, they just might have won over the Court.

When the city's attorney tried to assert that the founders intended only to protect gun rights in the "military context," Kennedy dropped on the city what was, by Supreme Court standards, a bomb: "It had nothing to do with the concern of the remote settler to defend himself and his family against hostile Indian tribes and outlaws, wolves and bears and grizzlies and things like that?"

This, for Heller and Neily and Levy, was even better than Kennedy's first comment. There was no way that a justice who understood the need of frontiersmen in the founding era to protect themselves with firearms was going to interpret the Second Amendment to apply only to militiamen. And so they were not at all surprised when, moments later, Justice Kennedy came right out and declared that in his view the Second Amendment "supplemented" the Constitution's other references to militias "by saying there's a general right to bear arms quite without reference to the militia either way."

Heller, Neily, and Levy each tried to keep straight faces and contain any expression of celebration in the courtroom. But the crestfallen faces of the city's supporters said it all. By the time oral argument ended, the result in *D.C. v. Heller* was all but official. With Kennedy's words and the dependable votes of the Court's other four conservatives, the amendment that had once been relegated to a footnote in constitutional law books was resurrected.

A New Day for the Second Amendment

After living for three decades in a city that had denied him the right to keep a handgun in his home to protect against his neighborhood's drug dealers and other purveyors of violent crime, Dick Heller returned to the same police station where his application had been stamped "Denied."[24]

This Monday morning in August of 2008, however, was quite different from that day six years earlier. In an opinion written by Justice

Scalia and released in June on the last day of the Court's term, the Supreme Court had restored the Second Amendment. The opinion declared that Americans like Dick Heller have a constitutional right to protect themselves and their homes and that the District of Columbia can't take that right away from them.

The Court's decision had been closely divided, with five votes for Heller and four justices vehemently dissenting. But five votes were enough. And on this Monday morning Dick Heller was holding the proof in his hands: an application to possess a pistol in his home.

The application was stamped, in big red letters, "Approved."

Thanks to the crusade launched when Robert Levy was persuaded to try to rescue the right to keep and bear arms, the Second Amendment has emerged from obscurity and longtime neglect. But Dick Heller's course of action need not be the only model we consider, because judges aren't the only people with the power to vindicate our rights. Legislators and presidents have a responsibility to protect the Constitution, and voters have the power to *require* those leaders to abide by it—all of it. Regardless of whether courts are willing to intervene, political leaders are oath bound to protect our government's founding document, and every time we go to the ballot box, "We the People" have the power to make every one of them abide by that oath.

CHAPTER 8

Reclaiming the Constitution Through Legislation

I WORK FOR A BRANCH OF GOVERNMENT THAT SERVES THE NA-
tion so poorly that, by some estimates, less than 10 percent of the
public approves of its job performance.[1] The nation has lost confidence in the men and women who point and shout from behind the
desks where Webster and Clay legislated and led. One recent poll of
Americans even indicated that Congress is more unpopular than
Vladimir Putin, for whom a mere 68 percent of respondents expressed a negative opinion.[2] And in a dangerous development, the
rest of the world is losing confidence in Congress too—a reality cap-
tured by the image of a crumbling U.S. Capitol building on the
cover of a recent issue of the academic journal *Foreign Affairs*.

Frustration and anger toward Congress are justified. Congress is
dysfunctional and out of touch. It is responsible for a bloated regulatory regime, a broken tax code, and an $18 trillion debt. It consis-
tently overpromises and underdelivers, claiming the capacity to cure
all that ails humanity but often exacerbating even the most basic
problems while trying to solve them.

In light of Congress's recent track record, it is tempting to think
it has no role to play in reviving the clauses of our Constitution that

our legislators have done so much to dismantle. It is tempting to look exclusively toward the courts to resurrect the Lost Constitution. After all, as the last chapter demonstrated, there is a role for courts to play in the restoration of our founding document.

But there are some problems that only Congress can solve. With regard to these areas, we have to count on our elected officials to enact serious, structural reforms, not because members of Congress are our best hope but because, in some areas, they are our only hope.

One of the areas in which Congress has the greatest potential to restore the Constitution's carefully crafted checks and balances concerns the regulatory (de facto lawmaking) powers of executive agencies. As described in chapter 3, by driving up prices on goods and services and lowering wages and employment, the federal regulatory system imposes a hidden $2 trillion tax on hardworking Americans every year. These regulations are written and enforced entirely by executive agencies. But the single biggest problem with our federal regulatory system is not the regulatory bodies themselves. The bigger problem is Congress.

It is the job of Congress to make laws. And with the task of making laws comes the daunting and painstaking responsibility of drawing lines. Congress has for too long delegated that task to others. By so doing, Congress has made it far too easy for its members to take credit for policies that are popular (*e.g.*, "Let's have clean air") while distancing themselves from policies that are unpopular (*e.g.*, "Let's adopt these strict, specific limits on greenhouse-gas emissions, even though the cost of electricity will necessarily skyrocket as a result of those limits"). The biggest problem with that is that, when those who are making the law don't *ever* stand for election—much less every two years (like representatives) or every six years (like senators)—no one can be held accountable.

Unfortunately, there is no reason to believe the courts can or will lead the way in reforming this blight on our constitutional system. Very few who have served on the Supreme Court in recent decades have expressed any willingness to reconsider the decades-old precedents that permit almost unlimited delegation to executive agencies. And even if a majority of the Court were willing to reconsider those precedents, the Court's options would be limited. Short of highly disruptive options like declaring all agency rule making unconstitutional, the Court would have to create a compromise rule with little textual support in the Constitution and little defense against critics accusing the Court of imposing a legislative compromise from the bench.

Fortunately, Congress can create a compromise rule with the potential to vastly improve this situation. In fact, the compromise was recently introduced in Congress. Formally titled the Regulations from the Executive in Need of Scrutiny Act, the REINS Act would treat all new "major rules"—that is, those federal regulations that would impose a "significant economic impact" of $100 million or more—essentially as legislative proposals that could take effect *only if enacted into law by Congress*. Under the REINS Act, each new major rule would receive expedited, fast-track consideration by both houses of Congress and, if passed, would then be forwarded to the president for his signature (or veto).

Here's why the REINS Act is necessary: Congress needs to be stripped of one of its favorite tricks—delegating broad lawmaking power to executive-branch agencies and then disclaiming any responsibility for the laws resulting from that delegation. It was with good reason that the founders put the lawmaking power in the hands of Congress, and the people suffer when Congress chooses to delegate that power to others—especially when the "others" are not accountable to the people.

Although the REINS Act currently has far more support from

Republicans than from Democrats (which isn't terribly surprising, given that the White House is currently occupied by a Democrat), it is a proposal that is neither liberal nor conservative. It is neither Democratic nor Republican. It is simply a commonsense idea, an *American* idea, whose time has come.

In fact, this is an idea whose time came long ago, when it was originally put forward by a very prominent Democrat who helped *create* the very system the REINS Act is designed to reform. In 1938 James Landis—a prominent adviser to FDR who assisted in the New Deal's creation of the modern federal regulatory system (and later served as dean of Harvard Law School)—became the first advocate of the kind of approach that we now associate with the REINS Act. Landis was dangerously enthusiastic about delegation, but even Landis believed that executive-branch agency regulations should be subject to approval by Congress because, according to him, "It is an act of political wisdom to put back upon the shoulders of Congress responsibility for controversial choices."[3]

That is the essence of the REINS Act.

Those opposed to the REINS Act have offered up several arguments. Perhaps the most common argument against it focuses on the fact that Congress lacks the kind of specialized knowledge that can be found in great abundance in our federal bureaucracies and that Congress simply cannot be entrusted with responsibility for regulating everything from power-plant emissions to the display of nutritional information on a box of Cap'n Crunch.

Those who raise this argument have a point, but that point cannot carry the day. It is true that executive-branch agencies are staffed with highly specialized, well-trained, and hardworking men and women who know a lot about their respective areas of expertise. That knowledge would not be lost under the REINS Act. Federal regulators would still have the power to *propose* new regulations. But those regulations, which would be presented to Congress on a fast track to an "up or down" vote, would take effect only if Congress agreed.

Others have argued that, with all of the regulations put forward each year by executive-branch agencies, Congress could not possibly be expected to cast enough votes to address each and every new major rule. That simply is not true. Over the last decade, federal agencies have issued an average of about sixty new major rules each year. While significant, this number is not so daunting as to make the REINS Act unworkable. At most, an additional sixty votes each year might be a mild inconvenience for a Congress that has already delegated far too much of its lawmaking authority.

In any event, the possibility that Congress might have to cast more votes under the REINS Act—even if it meant *hundreds* of additional votes each year—is hardly an argument against this necessary reform. Quite to the contrary, that is an argument *for* the REINS Act. If unelected, unaccountable bureaucrats are adding so many new laws to the books each year that the people's elected representatives in Congress cannot keep up with them, then we really do have a problem—one that is far more serious than concerns about Congress's workload.

Indeed, the sheer complexity of our legal system presents one of the greatest potential threats to liberty and prosperity. As James Madison described in *Federalist 62,* "It will be of little avail to the people, that the laws are made by men of their own choice, if the laws be so voluminous that they cannot be read, or so incoherent that they cannot be understood; if they be repealed or revised before they are promulgated, or undergo such incessant changes that no man, who knows what the law is today, can guess what it will be tomorrow. Law is defined to be a rule of action; but how can that be a rule, which is little known, and less fixed?"

When one examines the Code of Federal Regulations, one sees a legal regime that would be nothing short of horrifying to James

Madison. Not only is our federal regulatory system replete with laws that are "so voluminous that they cannot be read" (and in many cases "so incoherent that they cannot be understood"), but it cannot even be described as a system of laws "made by men [and women] of [our] own choice"!

Although the REINS Act would not fix the problem in its entirety,[4] it would go a long way toward putting the American people back in charge of the laws by which they are governed.

That kind of self-government was revolutionary in 1776.

In the twenty-first century, it should not be controversial.

Another problem requiring legislative reform is the balance between our need to collect data about foreign terrorists for national-security reasons and our Constitution's commitment to the basic privacy of innocent Americans. This field is particularly difficult for the courts to regulate because litigants cannot challenge a government action unless they have been injured by it, and when the government spies on Americans *in secret*, they cannot know—or prove—they have been injured.

But where the courts are often powerless to resurrect the Fourth Amendment's proscription against domestic spying, Congress isn't. That's why I have worked on a number of proposals to rein in and reform government surveillance.

One such measure is the USA Freedom Act, which I cosponsored in 2014 with Senator Pat Leahy (D-Vermont), who was at the time serving as chairman of the Senate Judiciary Committee. This important bill would prohibit the government from operating a bulk-data collection program by requiring the government to use a narrow, specific selector term (such as a person or entity) when requesting metadata from phone companies. It would give recipients of so-called National Security Letters (sweeping orders through which government agents may secretly request information from American citizens under the PATRIOT Act) increased rights to challenge the secrecy of those orders. And it would increase government transparency in a number of ways, including by requiring the government to make available the (currently secret) opinions issued by the FISA Court that render significant legal interpretations affecting privacy.

But acting defensively to protect against government abuse is not enough. We must also push forward to reform antiquated laws and protect privacy in an increasingly digitized age. We store our personal papers and information on our private lives in e-mail messages. Nonetheless, under current law, an e-mail is presumed to be abandoned after only 180 days, at which time the government has a statutory right to read it.

This is not right. I do not believe that the privacy interest that each American citizen has in her e-mail ends 180 days after she writes it, so Senator Leahy and I have introduced legislation to amend the Electronic Communications Privacy Act of 1986 to give e-mail the protection it deserves. Our bipartisan proposal would require the government to obtain a search warrant specific to an individual and backed by probable cause before the government can obtain that individual's e-mails and other digital data.

Even though it would take little more than a few acts of Congress to begin to resurrect some of the most important and most neglected parts of the Lost Constitution, passing these reforms through Congress will not be easy. Many members of Congress have a perverse incentive to keep the status quo exactly as it is. The delegation of Congress's legislative powers makes Congress's job simpler and makes it far easier for members of Congress to claim undue credit, avoid criticism where criticism is due, and remain in office in perpetuity. No congressmen wake up in the morning, look in the mirror, and ask themselves, *What can I do to make my reelection less likely?*

If anything, the pressures on legislators against protecting privacy are even stronger than those that keep Congress delegating away power. The reason is simple: fearmongering. On the question of balancing national security and individual privacy, the press, the executive branch, and even respected conservative thinkers frequently attempt to scare legislators into surrendering our most fundamental constitutional rights. They focus exclusively on the national-security consequences of government *inaction* while ignoring the constitutional implications of government *action*. And when that doesn't work, they resort to yelling.

I had been in the Senate only a few weeks when a bill to reauthorize the PATRIOT Act came before us. I had serious reservations about the Bush-era law, passed shortly after 9/11, but I wanted to make sure I understood the arguments before casting my vote.

I received multiple briefings from two very knowledgeable staff members employed by the Senate Select Committee on Intelligence, who patiently and professionally answered every question I presented to them. To accommodate my schedule, these two staffers even agreed to a meeting after the Senate had completed its votes on the evening of February 14, 2011. When I remembered that it was Valentine's Day, I told them the meeting could wait until later that week, acknowledging that there are few Valentine's Day activities *less* romantic than briefing a U.S. senator on the PATRIOT Act. But they insisted that what we were discussing was sufficiently important that their personal plans for the evening could be put on hold for an hour or so, and the meeting went forward as planned. I did, however, make sure that it didn't last too long.

Although some of what they told me confirmed (and in some cases even compounded) my preexisting concerns about the PATRIOT

Act, I was legally prohibited from publicly discussing much of what I learned during these briefings. The most troubling details, to my great frustration, were classified.

To their credit, the two very knowledgeable and professional Intelligence Committee staffers who briefed me did not resort to fear-mongering. When I inquired into the constitutional permissibility of the surveillance activities they were describing, they responded by carefully addressing the constitutional issues at play. I didn't agree with all of their conclusions, but their willingness to address constitutional concerns head on was refreshing.

At the end of one of our conversations, they asked whether I would be interested in speaking with a prominent lawyer—one whose name is probably familiar to many who will read this book—who had served in several high-profile positions within the federal government and was intimately familiar with the PATRIOT Act and the government programs that rely on its provisions. That lawyer, the Intelligence Committee staffers assured me, could help address my constitutional questions. They helped arrange for a phone call with him.

Although I had looked forward to the call, I was sorely disappointed in its outcome. While conversing with the man who had been identified as an expert on both the Constitution and the PATRIOT Act, I realized that his arguments were focused overwhelmingly not on the law or on the Constitution but on fear.

At some point during the conversation, I confided in this lawyer (who seemed to be assuming that I would vote to reauthorize the PATRIOT Act) that I hadn't made a final decision as to how I was going to vote. I identified a few constitutional concerns I had with the legislation and with its implications for the privacy of Americans.

The man on the other end of the phone didn't seem interested at all in talking about the Constitution or about the privacy interests underlying the Fourth Amendment. Each time I raised a constitutional question, he responded with a fear-based argument. While being careful not to show my growing frustration with his refusal to respond directly to my concerns, I calmly explained that, while I understood the reasons put forward for the PATRIOT Act after 9/11, I could not simply overlook the constitutional issues at stake. "I think I'd regret it if this law resulted in an abuse of power five or ten years down the road," I explained.

This statement seemed to kindle outrage in the man who, I now understood, was aggressively lobbying for the PATRIOT Act's reauthorization. He shouted, *"Well, I think I'd regret it if I looked out of my window and saw airplanes crashing into buildings!!!"*

Although I hardly knew this man (that is, beyond his unusually impressive résumé and his outstanding public-service record), I was as surprised as I was disappointed by his rage-filled reaction to what I thought were legitimate questions. At that moment I knew he wasn't interested in engaging in a meaningful discussion of the Constitution. I politely but promptly ended the phone call, thanking the man for his time and concern.

Then I voted against the PATRIOT Act.

I was among the very few Republicans to do so, just as I was among only a few Republicans to vote against extending the FISA Amendments Act. In recent years I have also been on the losing side of a series of amendments that I proposed with other civil-liberties advocates such as Senator Rand Paul (R-Kentucky) and Senator Dick Durbin (D-Illinois) that would have begun to restore the balance between privacy and security that the Fourth Amendment demands.

I am, however, undeterred. I believe passionately that privacy from undue government intrusion is a constitutional matter of the highest concern, just as I believe true self-government requires that elected representatives, rather than unaccountable bureaucrats, write our laws. Even though too many of my colleagues have yet to afford proper weight to these aspects of liberty, that will change when the American people make it change—either by changing their representatives' minds or by changing their representatives.

CHAPTER 9

Reclaiming the Constitution Through the Power of the Purse

In ADDITION TO THE POWER TO ENACT IMPORTANT REFORMS like the REINS Act and the USA Freedom Act, Congress has another time-honored power to exercise when it needs to stop an overreaching executive. It is a power wielded far too infrequently in recent years. And it is a power that James Madison described in *Federalist 58* as "the most complete and effectual weapon with which any constitution can arm the immediate representatives of the people, for obtaining a redress of every grievance, and for carrying into effect every just and salutary measure."

Madison was talking about the power of the purse. Without congressional approval, no federal program can be funded, and without funding, no program can be implemented. By simply refusing to fund a president's unconstitutional conduct, Congress can stop him dead in his tracks—even after courts have abdicated their responsibility to do so.

I was reminded of this principle on July 2, 2013—a year after the Supreme Court abdicated its responsibility in its review of

Obamacare. I was in my office in Salt Lake City when a member of my staff told me to turn on the news. What I saw was shocking. According to the report, President Obama had decided to delay Obamacare's "employer mandate," which requires many businesses to provide their employees with health insurance. Even though the legislation pushed through Congress and signed into law by President Obama himself required the employer mandate to kick in at the beginning of 2014, the president was delaying this provision's effective date by a year. In a stunning act of glib indifference, the Treasury Department announced the delay in a blog post.[1]

I immediately had three thoughts. First, this was outrageously unfair. The president was making hardworking men and women comply with the individual mandate, which requires individuals who do not want to buy health insurance to purchase it anyway. But President Obama wasn't willing to make powerful businesses suffer in the same way. Instead, undoubtedly after intense lobbying, the president was throwing a big bone to corporate America.

Second, this was a shamelessly partisan move, one that appeared to have been motivated by a desire to help the president's political party avoid an impending political backlash. Almost everyone understood that the employer mandate would likely result in considerable job losses, as some businesses would choose to lay off workers rather than provide them with already-expensive health insurance that would become significantly *more* expensive as a result of Obamacare. If the employer mandate took effect at the beginning of 2014, the resulting job losses could easily prove devastating for Democrats in 2014's midterm elections. What better way for the president to insulate Democrats from Obamacare's job-killing provisions than to delay one of its biggest burdens on job creation until *after* the 2014 election cycle?

Third, this was illegal. There was absolutely no statutory authority in Obamacare permitting the president to rewrite the provision prescribing the starting date for the employer mandate. Nor did President Obama have any inherent constitutional authority to do so. Quite to the contrary, the Constitution's text and structure make clear that a president lacks the authority to rewrite legislation unilaterally, *i.e.*, without any action by Congress. The first clause of the Constitution's first article is as simple as it is clear; it provides, "All legislative Powers herein granted shall be vested in a Congress of the United States, which shall consist of a Senate and House of Representatives." In other words, the power to legislate—that is, the power to *make law*—belongs to Congress. When the president rewrites acts of Congress, he usurps Congress's "legislative powers," upsets the Constitution's balance of power, and turns citizens into subjects by denying their directly elected representatives the exclusive authority to make the laws that govern their lives.

By delaying the employer mandate, President Obama had committed an unfair, partisan, and illegal act in open defiance of the Constitution. The question now squarely before me and my colleagues in Congress was . . . what to do about it. If the president's audacity went unchecked, it would only encourage him to repeat it. Congress needed to use its "most complete and effectual weapon"—its power over the federal purse.

On countless occasions throughout history, Congress has exercised this power. Sometimes Congress will authorize a program but then refuse to fund it. Other times it has funded programs for a while and later defunded them. For example, about a decade after it authorized the Vietnam War through the Gulf of Tonkin Resolution, Congress ended the war by cutting off funds.[2] Similarly, in the early 1980s Congress cut off funding that had once been available for President Reagan's support of anticommunist Contras fighting the left-wing government in Nicaragua.[3] As recently as President Obama's first term, Congress reversed course on where to store the nation's nuclear waste; it had previously funded a project to build a repository in Nevada's Yucca Mountain, but after an onslaught of pressure spearheaded by Nevada's Senator Harry Reid, Democrats succeeded in defunding the program.[4]

In fact, two years before President Obama began rewriting his signature legislative accomplishment, one of Obamacare's many provisions had itself been the subject of a successful defunding effort. As originally enacted in 2010, Obamacare created a program to encourage the formation of nonprofit start-up companies that would sell health insurance. The act appropriated $6 billion for loans and grants for those start-ups.[5] In 2011 Congress realized that much of that money was going to be wasted or unspent. Accordingly, Congress defunded the program by $2.2 billion.[6]

After giving the question a great deal of thought, discussing it with my team, and raising the matter with a number of my Republican colleagues, I decided there was only one appropriate response to the president's decision to illegally rewrite Obamacare: We had to make a serious effort to defund it for at least one year. If the president believed the law was not ready to be implemented as written, then we should take him at his word. At a minimum, we should not force the American people to pay for the law's implementation. To do so would reward the president in his flagrant defiance of the Constitution, encourage him and his successors to repeat such abuses in the future, and subject countless Americans to a terribly unpopular, plainly unconstitutional, and exorbitantly expensive upheaval of the relationship between citizens and their doctors, their insurers, and their government.

The "Defund Obamacare" movement was intuitively appealing to millions of Americans. Before long, millions had signed letters asking their senators and congressmen not to vote for any spending bill that spent money on Obamacare. Supporters ran advertisements on television, radio, and the Internet urging members of Congress to join our movement. And the Republican majority in the House of Representatives passed a spending measure that funded every federal program—at current levels, no less—except Obamacare. This represented a serious compromise gesture, given that Republicans were offering to maintain current funding levels for nearly every program in the federal constellation, including countless programs that Republicans have traditionally opposed.

In a letter I wrote to Senate Majority Leader Harry Reid on behalf of myself and a few colleagues in the Senate, we informed Senator Reid of our intention to oppose "legislation that funds further implementation or enforcement of ObamaCare." We wrote that the "president cannot seriously expect to waive ObamaCare's onerous mandates on large businesses, while simultaneously forcing individuals and families to pay to implement an individual mandate the public has opposed since before the law was even passed."

By late September 2013, America's political leaders had a choice to make. If October 1 arrived before Congress funded the government for the next fiscal year, countless federal programs would run out of money. The question was: Would Congress pass a spending bill amenable to the House, the Senate, and the president before October 1, and would such a measure include funding for Obamacare?

The question was complicated by an obscure but remarkably significant change in how Congress has allocated funds in recent years. Congress has historically funded the federal government first by passing a budget and then by enacting a series of spending measures (a dozen or so), each of which appropriates money for a different government function (*e.g.*, defense or transportation). When Congress follows this time-honored process, each spending measure is independently proposed by a committee, debated on the floor, amended, voted on, and sent to the president for his signature. This process has a way of keeping spending discussions in Congress focused. For example, it helps create an environment in which decisions regarding defense-related spending will be influenced by concerns related to national defense, not national parks, and decisions regarding national parks will be influenced by concerns related to national parks, not national defense.

This process was even more important in the context of Obamacare. Americans were about to come face to face with a law that would fundamentally alter their relationship with the federal government while putting their jobs and their existing health-care options at risk. The president himself had acknowledged that the law was not ready to be implemented as written. Meanwhile, a majority of Americans had never supported this law. Under the circumstances, it seemed especially important to have Obamacare funded (or not funded) based on the merits of Obamacare and not on the merits of other, more trusted programs (*e.g.*, national defense or national parks). Funding for Obamacare needed to be discussed, debated, and voted on by Congress based on what Americans thought of *Obamacare* and not based on what they thought about national parks, defense spending, veterans' benefits, or the day-to-day operations of any other government program. Had Congress simply followed its own appropriations process, it would have been far easier to have an open, honest debate regarding the merits of Obamacare.

Congress, however, has been disregarding that process since 2009. Instead of budgeting and then proposing, debating, amending, and passing a series of smaller spending bills, Congress has been keeping the government funded through a single, enormous, all-or-nothing spending package. If the giant bill becomes law, the government stays funded. If it is voted down or vetoed, some of the government shuts down.

This flagrant departure from the traditional budgeting and appropriations process has put our country on a collision course with disaster. Congress routinely spends money it doesn't have—creating trillion-dollar deficits—because senators and congressmen are afraid to vote against an all-or-nothing spending package, knowing that its defeat could result in a government shutdown. Meanwhile, meaningful oversight of the executive branch has become impossible because, without voting against funding the entire government, members of Congress can no longer say, "Hey, you're running this particular program poorly, so we're going to cut back on funding it until you get your act together!"

In the fight to defund Obamacare, President Obama wasted no time exploiting this departure from Congress's traditional spending practices. He steadfastly opposed any function-by-function approach to funding the government. He vowed to veto anything other than one, huge bill. And he mandated that the bill must include funding for Obamacare. That was one mandate he was *not* willing to delay.

When I heard the president's imperious veto threat, I wasn't just angered; I was saddened. Was the president really willing to shut down national parks, furlough civilian workers at the Department of Defense, and bring the wheels of countless federal agencies to a halt, just because he was unwilling to have funding for Obamacare debated and voted upon based on the merits of that (increasingly unpopular) law, which the president himself acknowledged was not ready to be implemented as written? *This,* I thought to myself, *is extortive.* This is unfairly punitive to the people. This is bad governance. This is tragic.

Unfortunately, after the president made his veto threat, the Democratic Senate majority leader made matters even worse. He announced that he wouldn't even allow the Senate to vote on the House's spending bill, which funded every federal program other than Obamacare. Now, not only was the president extorting Congress; the Senate's leader was helping him undermine the separation of powers.

The result of the president's intransigence was a painful and avoidable kind of chaos: At the stroke of midnight on October 1, the federal government ran out of money. Nonessential federal employees were furloughed. Visas and passport applications were not processed. Head Start programs went on hiatus. National parks, national museums, and national cemeteries were closed.[7]

At the same time, all "essential" government workers were kept on the job. That means around three quarters of the federal workforce kept working.[8] Air traffic controllers continued to keep the skies safe. Social security checks were signed and sent. The border was still patrolled (though apparently not secured). The NSA continued to monitor phone calls. The navy's ships still sailed, and the air force's planes still flew. Postal workers still delivered your mail.[9] Federal regulators even managed to create over a hundred federal regulations, adding more regulations in a week than they had ever added when the government was operating at full capacity.[10]

The conventional term for this state of affairs is a government "shutdown," even though most of the government isn't shut down. The important parts of most Americans' lives are not affected. That fact, however, provides cold comfort to those whose lives are adversely affected, and the public-relations effect of a shutdown can be dire for whichever party is blamed for it.

Sensing that he would succeed in blaming Republicans for the stalemate, President Obama went out of his way to make the shutdown as painful as possible. For example, while allowing a liberal protest on the National Mall for immigration reform, the administration spent large amounts of money erecting and manning barricades around the World War II Memorial on the National Mall to keep out visiting World War II veterans who might never have another chance to see the monument to their heroism. Huge amounts of money, which could have been spent running Head Start programs or processing passport applications, were spent keeping people *out* of national parks, forests, and recreation areas, intentionally hurting people in states like mine where most of the land is owned by the federal government. The Obama administration even padlocked swings at public parks in federal enclaves like Washington, D.C.

Just a few days into the shutdown, it was clearly hurting far more people than necessary, precisely because it was designed by the president to hurt as many people as possible. It was a shameless and expensive exercise in political manipulation and extortion.

Nevertheless, I still believed, even after the Democrats refused to compromise and the president shut down the government on October 1, that some sort of victory was possible. The American people didn't want a government shutdown, and they didn't want Obamacare. Far more Americans would have been outraged if they had understood that Democrats were shutting down the government in order to fund Obamacare, and they would have insisted that Democrats end the shutdown by agreeing to defund Obamacare. But unfortunately and unjustly, blame for the shutdown fell on Republicans—specifically, on those of us who were part of the defund-Obamacare effort.

The reason was simple. The president has a bully pulpit unequaled in size and effect by any other platform in Washington. This president, in particular, has at his disposal a compliant press corps that is all too willing to blame Republicans for anything and everything. In this case, that press corps was especially quick to blame Republicans for the government shutdown.

I thought this was tragic. Obamacare was on track to kill jobs, reduce wages, raise taxes, explode spending, hurt competition, inflate premiums, cancel popular insurance plans, and force religious people to fund contraceptives that violate their sincerely held beliefs. But because the public's blame for the shutdown was successfully diverted and foisted on Republicans by President Obama, the Washington establishment, and the mainstream media, the American people never received a clear message that Democrats—who refused to allow funding for Obamacare to be debated on its own merits— were responsible for the government shutdown.

As a result, political pressure built and built on the Republican House to pass a spending bill that would fund every federal program, including Obamacare. When it finally did, the Senate did what its Democratic majority had always wanted to do—fund Obamacare, claim credit for ending the government shutdown, and get back to business as usual in Washington.

When the shutdown ended, furloughed federal workers received back pay. National parks and monuments reopened. The padlocks were removed from swing sets in Washington's parks. The "Panda Cam" came back on at the National Zoo.

But regrettably, some things would never be the same. Obamacare's exchanges became operational in 2014. Its regulations became law. Its spending added to the debt. Its taxes slowed economic growth. Its punishment of work and wages cost jobs and reduced salaries. And, perhaps worst of all, its vast and complicated system of health care was imposed on millions of Americans. The funding of Obamacare unleashed on America a dangerous and disastrous genie, and it will be far more difficult to get the genie back in the bottle than it would have been to simply keep the bottle's lid shut.

At the same time, the defeat of the Defund-Obamacare movement ensured that President Obama's lawlessness would continue and expand. In the months since then, the president changed the deadline to buy health insurance; postponed the starting date for the small business exchange; ordered states to allow people to keep canceled insurance plans; expanded subsidies to cover enrollees not covered under the statute; extended the deadline for the expiration of high-risk insurance pools; pushed back the enrollment period in 2014 until after the midterm elections; delayed enforcement of the law's ban on discrimination by employers against low-level workers; extended the deadline (for the third time) for the Pre-Existing Condition Insurance Plan; and once again delayed part of the employer mandate.[11]

By late 2014, after President Obama had repeatedly usurped Congress's authority and rewritten Obamacare dozens of times, it was clear that we were not well positioned to stop his assault on the Constitution. At least for the time being, he had won, and we had lost; rule by executive fiat had won, and the separation of powers had lost; the transformation of the relationship between the government and the governed had won, and the Constitution's creation of a federated structure with enumerated and limited powers had lost.

This was, however, only a single battle. The larger war for the Constitution goes on. As long as our government remains in the hands of fallible humans, some of them will seek perpetually to expand and even abuse their power. At the same time, the Constitution will stand ready to restrain those individuals and protect our liberty—if only we are willing to fight for it.

CHAPTER 10

What *You* Can Do to Reclaim the Constitution

WHEN THE STATE OF NEW YORK OPENED ITS CONVENTION TO ratify the Constitution in June 1788, few states were more important to the union's success than the Empire State. Yet in few other states did ratification appear more improbable—because New Yorkers had a lot to lose. The new Constitution would make customs duties, the state's most lucrative revenue stream, a national tax. It would also allow Congress to force New Yorkers help pay other states' war debts, even though New Yorkers had already paid off their own debt. It's no wonder that New York voters sent to the convention nineteen supporters of the Constitution . . . and forty-six opponents.[1]

Against these almost impossible odds, New York's Alexander Hamilton defended the Constitution section by section and clause by clause. At the national convention in Philadelphia, he had sometimes stumbled. But at the ratifying convention in Poughkeepsie— and in the *Federalist Papers* written to shift public opinion across the state—he was masterful.

After the first week of debate was filled with Anti-Federalists' forceful and emotional attacks on the Constitution, Hamilton pleaded for a "cool examination" of the instrument in question. The understandable "doubts . . . suspicions, and speculations" of opponents were based on centuries of central governments trampling on the rights of their people. But the United States was different, because "we have formed a constitution upon free principles." Among them was the principle of "free representation." Never in America would its people need to fear an out-of-control government. In America, most federal legislators "hold their offices two years, and then return to their constituents." Here, said Hamilton, the constituents are always in charge. "Here, sir, the *people* govern."[2]

Hamilton had come a long way from his proposal in Philadelphia for an elected monarch (although he had never been opposed to a popularly elected House of Representatives). And in the end, the New York ratifying convention was persuaded by the power of his arguments—and by the promise of a bill of rights. On July 26, by just three votes, the convention in Poughkeepsie ratified the United States Constitution. In a celebratory parade through New York City produced by the Constitution's supporters, a twenty-seven-foot-long float in the shape of a frigate sailed through the streets of Manhattan. The ship was called the *Hamilton*.

Hamilton's words—"Here, sir, the people govern"—capture the reason why the Lost Constitution will never be a lost cause. In the United States the people always ultimately have the power to rein in, redirect, or kick out their elected representatives. They need only marshal the political will to do so.

As the previous three chapters showed, Congress and the courts each have a role to play in reclaiming the Constitution. But if we wait around for them to act on their own initiative, we will be waiting forever. The Second Amendment was not resurrected until advocates like Clark Neily, Robert Levy, and Dick Heller forced the courts to resurrect it. The REINS Act and the USA Freedom Act will not pass until constituents force their representatives to pass them. And Congress will never use its power over the purse to reclaim the Constitution unless voters elect legislators who understand our founding charter and are committed to respecting it.

Reclaiming our constitutional principles therefore begins with the American voter. Only we can force our government officials to obey their oaths to preserve, protect, and defend the Constitution. Only we can reshape our nation's attitudes, actions, and elections in a way that will restore the Lost Constitution.

Attitudes

First we have to influence the attitudes of those around us, making every effort to persuade our friends, neighbors, colleagues, aunts, and uncles (even the crazy ones who we think will never listen) that constitutionally limited government not only matters but is essential to our prosperity as a nation and to our way of life. Ronald Reagan made a similar point in 1977 when he explained that "[i]f we truly believe in our principles, we should sit down and talk." He implored those who share our values to "[t]alk with anyone, anywhere, at any time if it means talking about the principles" of constitutionally limited government.[3]

Doing this will require some reading and thinking—and ultimately a whole lot of talking—but it will work. We have to persuade others that the processes and personnel through which laws are made, enforced, and interpreted matter. Many around you won't care, at least initially, about the fact that some of the procedures established by the Constitution are not being followed. A lot of people are inclined to dismiss departures from the Constitution as a kind of harmless error. This is where analogies can help.

If you have friends who claim not to care whether this or that aspect of the Constitution is being circumvented in Washington, try making a comparison to something smaller and more familiar. Ask your friends to imagine, for example, that their local homeowners' association was created for three limited purposes: to ensure the adequacy of street lights, to provide for the maintenance of parks and other common areas, and to arrange for the weekly removal of garbage. Ask your friends to imagine further that the association is governed by a seven-member board chosen at an annual meeting of the association's members and that, once elected, the board is empowered to make all decisions affecting the association with one exception: Any decision to increase the monthly fees paid by homeowners must be approved at the annual homeowners' association meeting. Finally, ask your friends to imagine that the association's seven-member board decided to increase the monthly fees paid by homeowners by 25 percent without seeking approval from the association's members and to begin imposing fines on homeowners who failed to keep their dogs behind a fence or on a leash. Alternatively, ask them to imagine that the association's seven-member board adopted a nutritional-standards rule requiring each homeowner to certify in writing each month that all of the occupants of his or her home are consuming at least two servings of green vegetables each day.

My guess is that, to one degree or another, your friends would express some outrage if their homeowners' association did any of these things, especially given that each action outlined above would plainly not be authorized by the association's own rules. Most of your friends would never stand for such excesses.

If they wouldn't allow their *homeowners' association* to overstep the rules put in place to limit its own very narrow authority, why should they be willing to let their national government—which spends nearly twenty-five cents out of every dollar that moves through the American economy each year—do things it has no business doing and ignore the procedures it is required to follow? Once you have asked this question, you will have made significant progress in explaining the importance of limited government.

The next step is simple: Ask your friends and family to read the Constitution. It is short—with its amendments, it contains less than eight thousand words and can be read in its entirety in less than an hour. It is written in relatively plain, simple English. And it is still very, very relevant to what is going on in our country today.

Most important, reading the Constitution tends to change the way people think about the federal government, how it operates, and how it should operate. It prompts members of the public to view what happens in Washington not with blind faith or a resigned sense of powerlessness but with a healthy degree of skepticism and informed understanding. As people read and begin to understand the Constitution, they will start to see that—like the homeowners in the hypothetical scenario outlined above—those making decisions on their behalf are not always following the rules by which they are bound.

In short, if we want to restore the Constitution to its rightful place of prominence, we have to make sure that we (and those around us) know what's in it—because, as Justice Anthony Kennedy has said, "You cannot preserve what you do not revere. You cannot protect what you do not comprehend. You cannot defend what you do not know."[4]

Actions

As soon as people start caring about and developing an understanding of the Constitution, many of them will want to know what they can do to help restore constitutionally limited government. When this happens, tell them that the best thing they can do is to have conversations just like the one you've had with them. Challenge them to have such conversations with at least five people they know. This alone can make a big difference.

Those who care should also be encouraged to call or write to their senators and congressmen on issues that concern them, especially on issues of constitutional importance. When unelected bureaucrats promulgate a new, problematic regulation, voters should write to their elected representatives in Washington, reminding them that the power to make laws belongs to Congress, pointing out that federal regulations are costing the American economy roughly $2 trillion each year, and encouraging them to enact regulatory reform measures like the REINS Act, which would help put Congress back in charge of (and once again make Congress accountable for) the task of lawmaking.

In each instance, the message communicated to Washington needs to tie back to the Constitution, always focusing on the fact that, as long as that document remains in force, officials in Washington need to follow it. The message needs to remind elected officials that the Constitution's entire purpose is to *restrain* government power; absent such a purpose, we probably wouldn't need it. The message should also identify specific provisions of the Constitution that are at issue, paying special attention to big-picture constitutional restraints like separation of powers (think of the legislative powers clause, putting Congress, and not unelected bureaucrats, in charge of lawmaking) and federalism (think of the Tenth Amendment and Congress's limited powers).

The importance of emphasizing federalism cannot be overstated. We must continually remind our government officials and our fellow Americans that federal power is limited and that power not identified as federal by the Constitution is reserved to the states. This principle, we must explain, has the potential to give more Americans more of what they want from their government. Federalism, at its core, is neither liberal nor conservative; it is a principle that, where followed, allows diverse political viewpoints (which vary dramatically from one region to another) to be respected.

Consider the way Americans' feelings about socialized medicine vary from state to state. Many people in Vermont—perhaps a solid majority—would like to have a single-payer, government-funded, government-operated health-care system. By contrast, most people in Utah (my state) don't feel that way and would probably be more content with less government intervention in health care than with more.

In any event, the people in each state should have the chance to decide for themselves what kind of role they want the government to play in the provision of health-care services. If most people in Vermont want a form of socialized medicine, then they should be able to move in that direction. They would be able to do that far more effectively, completely, and promptly if only the federal government would get out of the way—that is, if only the federal government didn't already occupy so much of the government-funded-health-care arena that relatively little discretion remains with the states.

As it stands today, however, most of the people in Utah and most of the people in Vermont are *not* getting what they want in this area because far too many of their decisions are being made on a national level, rather than on a state-by-state basis. This wouldn't happen if those holding federal offices showed more respect for principles of federalism. They should do so, not just because federalism is required by the Constitution but also because federalism, when followed conscientiously, creates a system that allows people throughout the country to get more of what they want from their government and less of what they don't want.

Federalism, in short, protects our country's rich viewpoint diversity. We need to start embracing it and stop avoiding it. It will allow more Americans to have more of the kind of government they want.

Along the way, expect to encounter some resistance from those who have become convinced that having a big, powerful government—one that need not be restrained by an ancient document—is somehow a good thing. Be prepared to make the case that an unrestrained, all-powerful government isn't the answer to all of mankind's ailments and that such a government has the potential to make our problems much, much worse.

Elections

Finally, we have to bring our knowledge of the Constitution with us to the ballot box. And we have to vote differently—especially when it comes to federal offices.

More than at any point in the past, freedom-loving Americans should support only those candidates for federal office who have read, understand, and are deeply committed to the limited-government principles embodied in the Constitution. While this task may sound difficult, it's relatively easy to separate the wheat from the chaff once you know what questions to ask candidates seeking your vote.

To start the conversation with (or about) the candidate in question, begin by inquiring generally into what the candidate sees as the purpose of the federal government. Any answer that fails prominently to emphasize the limited nature of federal power—or that describes federal power in an open-ended fashion—is unsatisfactory.

Thus, if a candidate says that the federal government's purpose is "to ensure that Americans are prosperous and well educated," further inquiry is in order. Americans should, of course, be prosperous and well educated. But in this context, how we get there matters. When Congress does its job well, it helps us get to that place—not because Congress has the power to legislate into existence all of the precise means by which people become prosperous and well educated but because federal power properly exercised leaves individuals free to do what they do best without interference from (a) Congress or (b) the kinds of problems that Congress is duly and uniquely empowered to address. Congress has a defined role in American society and in our system of government, not an open-ended one. In that respect, Congress should rarely be in a position to claim credit or accept blame for the overall state of America's economy or for the quality of its education system.

If Congress is respecting the limited nature of its power, its primary impact on such things will be indirect. If, for example, Congress failed to make adequate provisions for our national defense, then both our economy and our education system would be placed at risk; but that does not mean that Congress can always claim credit or accept blame for the strength of the economy or the quality of public education throughout the country.

A candidate for federal office who promises the sun, moon, and stars should be viewed with a healthy degree of skepticism—especially if he or she fails even to attempt to square such promises with constitutional limitations on federal power. A satisfactory answer to a question about the nature of federal power will always entail some recognition that the federal government's powers are, as James Madison described them in *Federalist 45*, "few and defined," while those reserved to the states are "numerous and indefinite."

A good answer will summarize briefly the powers granted to Congress in Article I, Section 8, and elsewhere in the Constitution. At a minimum, such an answer should acknowledge that the powers of Congress extend to the regulation of commerce between the states and with foreign nations and the power to provide for our national defense.

A better answer will recognize that Congress has drifted considerably from the entire notion that it possesses only limited, enumerated powers. Such an answer should acknowledge the unmistakable connection among (a) the dramatic increase of federal spending as a percentage of GDP over the last eighty years, (b) the deferential standards of review applied by the Supreme Court in reviewing acts of Congress, and (c) Congress's failure to limit its own authority, independently of the Supreme Court.

The best answer will be one that provides specific examples of legislation that the candidate will oppose because they cannot be reconciled with the candidate's reading of the Constitution—even if the laws could withstand a constitutional challenge in court, based on the permissive standards established by misguided precedents.

Extra credit should be given to any candidate who acknowledges that members of Congress are required to take an oath to uphold the Constitution and that this oath binds lawmakers to do more than simply restrain their power to the extent they are ordered to do so by the Supreme Court.

Some people, including many self-described constitutionalists, respond to this point by insisting that it is, after all, the Supreme Court's job to interpret the Constitution. That statement may be true as far as it goes. When litigants bring a dispute to the attention of a court with jurisdiction over it, the judiciary will supply the interpretation as necessary to resolve the underlying dispute.

In countless other circumstances, however, the courts have no occasion even to consider questions of constitutional dimension. Parties disputing the proper interpretation of one or more words in the Constitution may, for instance, choose to resolve their dispute on their own, without ever asking the courts to get involved. Unless the courts are asked, no court will weigh in on the constitutional dispute at issue. And unless a court weighs in on the constitutional dispute, there will be no judicial precedent on the issue.

The absence of judicial intervention in these areas hardly obviates the need for officials in the political branches to consider the constitutional implications of their actions. Quite to the contrary; if anything, the fact that many disputes are *not* resolved by the courts only underscores the solemn duty of those who serve in the political branches of government to faithfully defend the Constitution.

For example, in impeachment proceedings, members of Congress understand they are the ultimate arbiters of whether the individual at issue has committed "treason, bribery, or other high crimes and misdemeanors." If that power has been abused, I am not aware of it.

I can't help but wonder whether the absence of abuse in this area has something to do with the fact that members of Congress understand that in this area, the buck really does stop with them. They can't rely on the federal courts to clean up any mistakes they might make. Perhaps when they feel a sense of ultimate stewardship and accountability, they act more responsibly.

If anything, I wonder whether Congress may have been too cautious in wielding the impeachment power, erring on the side of caution so much that presidents have been emboldened to act like kings. Many times I have been asked what Congress can do in response to an out-of-control executive. My response is that the Constitution has given Congress two tools to deal with this kind of problem: One is the withholding of funds, as discussed above; the other is impeachment.

When I worked at the U.S. Supreme Court, I occasionally had opportunities to show visitors around the building, which is a true (but often uncelebrated) architectural masterpiece. In preparing for such opportunities, I paid special attention to the symbolic architectural and artistic features of our nation's highest tribunal. I learned all I could about the building and its history.

This exercise gave additional meaning to my experience working at the Court. At times it seemed as though my work—which involved assisting Justice Alito as a law clerk—was somehow informed and enhanced by the symbols adorning the building. Those symbols underscore the sacred trust placed in government by the people, reminding jurists and visitors alike that human virtues and vices interact in a way that makes governing a complex and often risky endeavor. The stories told by those symbols inform the public of the

High Court's purpose and the role of law, justice, and jurisprudence in our society.

My experience at the Supreme Court has served as an informative backdrop to my time in the U.S. Senate, where, working at the Capitol (just across the street from the Court), my thoughts are unavoidably influenced by beautiful and poignant images presented on canvas and in wood, plaster, and stone. From one end of the Capitol to the other, the building is filled with depictions of liberty and all that our nation treasures, symbols of strength, wisdom, order, virtue, charity, and self-restraint. The symbols themselves, and all that they represent, make the Capitol not only aesthetically pleasing but also thought-provoking. In every corridor one can see eagles representing foresight and freedom, scales representing justice, scrolls and tablets representing our laws and our Constitution, and countless other symbols that are timelessly connected to the American psyche.

One sculpture, *Liberty and the Eagle* by Enrico Causici, consistently captures my attention and my imagination. I am drawn to it not only because of its inherent beauty and unique style but also because it incorporates so many symbols into a single work of art. Perched on a high ledge in the chamber used by the House of Representatives from 1807 to 1857, this sculpture combines multiple thematic elements representing the ideals of our nation and our form of government. The centerpiece of this work is a tall woman in flowing, regal robes—Liberty. The scroll she holds in her outstretched right hand is the U.S. Constitution, an instrument of liberty delivered by Liberty herself. To her right is an eagle, the high-flying symbol of American power, foresight, and freedom. At her left is a *fasces*, an ancient Roman symbol of strength consisting of a tightly bound bundle of sticks. Although each stick in the bundle is small and relatively weak on its own, the sticks become surprisingly strong when they are bound together; it's a common architectural representation of the phrase *E Pluribus Unum*, "Out of Many, One."

To me, the most fascinating part of *Liberty and the Eagle* is the creature coiled tightly around the *fasces*, as if holding it together: a snake. Every time I see this sculpture, I find the snake a little unsettling—in much the same way I feel queasy whenever and wherever I happen to see a snake, whether in my backyard, in the wilderness, or even in a glass cage at a zoo or pet store. Although this snake isn't real, I still find it startling to see it depicted as somehow holding our republic together.

Very few Americans, if asked what species of fauna or flora best represents the ideals of America, would identify *any* reptile, much less the snake. Culturally, we have come to associate the snake with deception. Regardless of the reasons, most Americans would probably agree that snakes are mysterious animals that, when used as symbols, send a message that is at best mixed.

With all of this in mind, I have often wondered what could possibly have convinced the sculptor of *Liberty and the Eagle* to feature the snake so prominently in a sculpture that, in every other respect, seems to capture so much of what is virtuous and admirable about America. Enrico Causici isn't here to give us his own explanation, so we are left to wonder on our own.

Given my own affinity for the biblical symbolism prevalent throughout the Capitol, my personal interpretation of this piece is influenced by the Bible. When I see this sculpture, I think of Jesus's admonition that his followers be "wise as serpents, and harmless as doves."[5]

When Jesus uttered those words, his listeners would likely have associated the serpent with the capacity to discern between good and evil. It was the serpent that convinced Adam and Eve to partake of the forbidden fruit—the fruit of "the tree of knowledge of good and evil," as described in Genesis—by promising them that if they did so they would "be as gods, knowing good and evil."[6] Telling his followers to be "wise as serpents" could thus have emphasized the need to be discerning and to be aware of and on the lookout for evils that might come among them.

This interpretation takes on additional meaning when one considers that the "wise as serpents" admonition was uttered as an addendum to Jesus's warning that his followers would sometimes be sent forth "as sheep in the midst of wolves."[7] This part of the Bible warns readers of a harsh reality: Those who are inclined to harm others sometimes fail to recognize that they might be surrounded by people who, contrary to their carefully managed appearances, are the opposite of innocent. Hence the need for Jesus's followers to be "wise as serpents" but "harmless as doves."

Perhaps *Liberty and the Eagle* sends a secular version of the same message. I wonder whether Enrico Causici wanted to remind Americans that, while most of us have high aspirations for good government, we must not allow ourselves to assume that the aspirations of those around us—particularly those who are elected to serve in the Capitol—are equally devoted to the noble principles upon which our country was founded.

If this interpretation is correct, then this serpent warns us that the system established by the Constitution will become subject to abuse, even by those who take oaths to protect it. The U.S. Constitution was written to make the men and women of America free. But it can succeed in protecting them only when it is followed, and only when the people take steps to prevent it from being distorted and ultimately used against them.

As a peace-loving people, we must be "harmless as doves." But as a people charged with the task of protecting ourselves from threats to our liberty, we must also be "wise as serpents."

What, then, do we need to watch out for as Americans? How can we identify our political "wolves"—those who threaten our freedom and form of government—even as they remain concealed behind "sheep's clothing"?

The founding generation understood that almost *anyone* entrusted with the levers of government power has the potential to become a wolf and that government officials must therefore be checked at every turn. In *Federalist 51*, James Madison gives us a good window into the founding generation's concerns in this area. Indeed, he suggested that the very need for the Constitution's system of checks and balances is itself "a reflection on human nature" and that government itself may properly be described as "the greatest of all reflections on human nature."

He went on to reason that "[i]f men were angels, no government would be necessary" and that "[i]f angels were to govern men, neither external nor internal controls on government would be necessary." But alas, Madison concluded, men are not angels and we have yet to find a way for angels to govern men. We must therefore "fram[e] a government which is to be administered by men over men," taking into account the harsh reality that human nature routinely causes men to abuse government power. This can be achieved only with great difficulty; we "must first enable the government to control the governed; and in the next place oblige it to control itself."

Federalist 51 points out that a republican form of government that holds public officials accountable through regular elections is itself not enough to prevent politicians from abusing their power. Elections naturally create within the government a "dependence on the people." Aware of this dynamic, public officials naturally seek to turn this relationship on its head by making the people dependent on government, thereby strengthening the tie between big government and the politicians who traffic in it. Thus, "experience has taught mankind the necessity of auxiliary precautions." In other words, we need checks on government power—including federalism and the separation of powers—that go above and beyond what can be achieved through regular elections.

Elections, in the absence of "auxiliary precautions," could actually enhance the risk that government officials will abuse their power by promoting the *appearance* that such officials are sheep—that their interests are seamlessly aligned with those of the people they represent. Meanwhile, elected officials rely increasingly on a familiar campaign message: "You need *me* to make government work for *you*." In spreading this message, they don't just mask their self-serving intentions; they obscure and diminish the Constitution by acting as if the lawmaker is more important than the law. They don't just disguise their role as marketers of corruption and dysfunction; they undermine the role of the Constitution by putting their own personality in its place. This explains why so many take an oath to honor the Constitution but then work tirelessly to weaken it. It is the Constitution itself that makes government work for the people, and that is why there is an oath to uphold it and a constant temptation by those in power to marginalize it.

I therefore see the snake in *Liberty and the Eagle* as a sobering reminder of the need for us as citizens to discern the difference between good and evil, between sheep and wolves masquerading as sheep, and between hardworking Americans sustaining constitutional principles and government officials wielding unchecked power. For too long the enemies of limited government have been winning this battle. While those who love freedom are coalescing in record numbers to mount a resistance, the struggle is far from over.

We are still the stewards of the country we have inherited, and we won't be fooled forever by the shenanigans of the ill intentioned or shortsighted. This nation is and will continue to be a light to all other nations, a treasure purchased by blood and built by the hearts, minds, and determination of its people. We will preserve what we value and understand, and the outcome of this process will shape the fate of our constitutionally protected republic for the better.

Although we have plenty of reasons to be concerned about our republic's state, I am nothing but optimistic about its fate. I am not like Jimmy Stewart's Mr. Smith, battling for a lost cause because "lost causes are the only causes worth fighting for." Nor am I as fatalistic as that great fighter for human freedom, Whittaker Chambers, who believed communists were on history's "winning side" and, with resignation, said "it is better to die on the losing side than to live under Communism."[8]

To be sure, the Constitution has taken a beating over the years, and restoring it is a daunting endeavor. Nevertheless, on our side are the values of the American people. We don't want Washington politicians taking away our right to self-defense. We don't want any but the most accountable representatives to have the power to raise our taxes. We don't want unelected bureaucrats imposing mountains of regulations with trillions of dollars of costs. We don't want federal judges barring all religious utterance from the public square. We don't want Big Brother snooping into our most private affairs. We don't want what the founding generation would never have ratified and what subsequent generations have never endorsed—a federal government of unlimited power.

Instead, as Americans, we desire a limited government of checks and balances that protect individual liberty. By the millions, we have an instinctive attraction to these principles. Because they form the backbone of this nation, the Constitution will always have a fighting chance.

Winston Churchill famously said, "Americans can always be counted on to do the right thing after they have exhausted all other possibilities." I'm not sure I can agree with the second half of that sentence, but I think we can accept the first half of it as a profound compliment. The American people *can always be counted on to do the right thing*.

George Washington expressed a similar sentiment in 1787. In a letter to his nephew, Bushrod Washington, expressing his confidence in the recently proposed Constitution, the future president wrote: "The power under the Constitution will always be in the people. It is entrusted for certain defined purposes, and for a certain limited period, to representatives of their own choosing; and whenever it is executed contrary to their interest, or not agreeable to their wishes, their servants can, and undoubtedly will, be recalled."[9]

What George Washington wrote in 1787 remains true today. Whenever we, as a people, decide that the Constitution is being "executed contrary to [our] interest" and in a manner "not agreeable to [our] wishes," we will start to care differently, act differently, and vote differently as we seek for the limitations on power that have been promised and yet are lost.

That vindication will begin when we embrace the opportunity for a real national discussion about the meaning of our Constitution. We must be patient but persistent. We must be honest about the meaning of the words written in the summer of 1787 and on subsequent occasions when the Constitution was amended. We must understand how their meaning has been forgotten. We must be able to point to the key passages of our nation's highest law, demand that our elected officials respect them, and hold each of those officials accountable for disregarding them.

I hope this book will be a part of the beginning of that conversation.

ACKNOWLEDGMENTS

With much appreciation to: Adrian Zackheim, Bria Sandford, and the entire team at Sentinel; Matt Latimer, Keith Urbahn, and Justin Walker at Javelin; and my entire family, with a special mention of my father, the late Rex E. Lee, an outstanding defender of the Constitution whose inspiration made this book possible.

NOTES

AUTHOR'S NOTE

1. Michael Shaara, *The Killer Angels* (New York: Ballantine Books, 1974), vii.

INTRODUCTION

1. Peter B. Gardner, "Brothers in Law," *BYU Magazine*, Spring 2011.
2. Ibid.

CHAPTER 1: Ducking and Dodging the Constitution

1. Eric Zimmerman, "Pelosi to Reporter: 'Are You Serious?'," *The Hill*, http://thehill.com/blogs/blog-briefing-room/news/64547-pelosi-to-reporter-are-you-serious
2. "George W. Bush: Statement on Signing the Bipartisan Campaign Reform Act of 2002," March 27, 2002, The American Presidency Project, http://www.presidency.ucsb.edu/ws/?pid=64503.
3. Ibid.

CHAPTER 2: The Compromise That Saved the Constitutional Convention . . . and That Should Have Saved Us from Obamacare

The main sources for this chapter are Max Farrand, *The Records of the Federal Convention of 1787*, Rev. ed. (New Haven: Yale University Press, 1966); Richard R. Beeman, *Plain, Honest Men: The Making of the American Constitution* (New York: Random House, 2009); and Lynne V. Cheney, *James Madison: A*

Life Reconsidered (New York: Viking Penguin, 2014). Much of the substance is taken from the history those sources describe.

1. Max Farrand (ed.), *The Records of the Federal Convention of 1787: Volume II*, Rev. ed. (New Haven: Yale University Press, 1966), 642-43.
2. Although inspired by the historical record, this scene is imagined.
3. Catherine Drinker Bowen, *Miracle at Philadelphia: The Story of the Constitutional Convention, May to September 1787* (Boston: Little, Brown, 1966), 14.
4. Ibid., 13–14.
5. Gordon Lloyd, "Introduction to the Constitutional Convention," *Teaching American History*, http://teachingamericanhistory.org/convention/intro/.
6. Lynne V. Cheney, *James Madison: A Life Reconsidered* (New York: Viking Penguin, 2014), 121.
7. Ibid., 125.
8. Farrand, *The Records of the Federal Convention of 1787: Volume I*, 21.
9. The quotes in this section and other sections of this chapter describing the Constitutional Convention combine and draw implications from the notes of Madison, Yates, and other note takers, which differ regarding the exact words speakers used. Those notes are compiled in *The Records of the Federal Convention of 1787*, edited by Max Farrand.
10. Erastus Howard Scott, ed. *The Federalist and Other Constitutional Papers by Hamilton, Jay, Madison and Other Statesmen of Their Time*, vol. 1 (Chicago: Scott, Foresman, 1898), 589 (quoting letter to Luther Martin from Oliver Ellsworth).
11. Bowen, *Miracle at Philadelphia*, 93.
12. Although inspired by the historical record, dialogue and details in this scene are imagined.
13. Farrand, *Records of the Federal Convention of 1787: Volume II*, 224.
14. Ibid.
15. Ibid., 273.
16. By its terms the Constitution required only nine states to ratify it. The ninth state, New Hampshire, ratified it on June 21, 1788. But as a practical matter the Constitution needed the support of powerful states like Virginia and New York, which did not ratify it until June 25, 1788 (Virginia), and July 26, 1788 (New York). The ratification process technically continued for several years, until May of 1790, when Rhode Is-

land became the final state to ratify the Constitution. But by then the Constitution had gone into effect.

17. "Remarks by the President at Rally on Health Insurance Reform," White House, Office of the Press Secretary, September 19, 2009, http://www.whitehouse.gov/the-press-office/remarks-president-rally -health-insurance-reform-college-park-md.

18. "Text of the Patient Protection and Affordable Care Act," Gov -Track.us, https://www.govtrack.us/congress/bills/111/hr3590/text/ ih; "H.R.3590: Patient Protection and Affordable Care Act," Library of Congress, http://beta.congress.gov/bill/111th-congress/house-bill/ 3590/all-actions-with-amendments/.

CHAPTER 3: From Congress to a King

The main sources for the section on Alexander Hamilton are Ron Chernow, *Alexander Hamilton* (New York: Penguin Press, 2004); and Joseph J. Ellis, *Founding Brothers: The Revolutionary Generation* (New York: Alfred A. Knopf, 2001).

1. Ken Burns, in his documentary on Thomas Jefferson, is among those who have pointed out how many—and how many types—of monarchs reigned in 1776. *Thomas Jefferson: A Film By Ken Burns* (1997).

2. Although Hamilton did confront a mob at King's College, much of the dialogue and many of the details in this scene are imagined.

3. Ron Chernow, *Alexander Hamilton* (New York: Penguin Press, 2004), 64.

4. The quotes in this section and other sections of this chapter describing Hamilton's address on June 18 to the Constitutional Convention combine and draw implications from the notes of Madison, Yates, King, and Hamilton, which differ regarding the exact words speakers used. Those notes are compiled in Max Farrand's *The Records of the Federal Convention of 1787: Volume II*, from pages 282 to 310.

5. Chernow, *Alexander Hamilton*, 229 (quoting William Pierce).

6. Maggie Riechers, "Honor Above All," *Humanities*, May/June 2007, Volume 28, Number 3, http://www.neh.gov/humanities/2007/may june/feature/honor-above-all.

7. In this scene, the details of the reactions of Hamilton's colleagues, including Franklin's sleep, are imagined.

8. "Transcript of Virginia Plan (1787)," www.ourdocuments.gov, http://www.ourdocuments.gov/doc.php?flash=true&doc=7&page=transcript. This is the version of the Virginia Plan as amended by the Committee of the Whole.

9. Quotations from President Roosevelt's First Inaugural Address in this chapter come from "Address by Franklin D. Roosevelt," Joint Congressional Committee on Inaugural Ceremonies, http://www.inaugural.senate.gov/swearing-in/address/address-by-franklin-d-roosevelt-1933.

10. Anne M. Cohler, Basia C. Miller, & Harold S. Stone (eds.), *Montesquieu: The Spirit of the Laws* (Cambridge: Cambridge University Press, 1989), 157.

11. David Schoenbrod, *Power Without Responsibility: How Congress Abuses the People Through Delegation* (New Haven: Yale University Press, 1993), 37.

12. Charles H. Koch Jr., "James Landis: The Administrative Process" *Administrative Law Review* 48 (1996): 419–33, available at http://scholarship.law.wm.edu/facpubs/633.

13. "New Deal Programs & Timeline," Living New Deal, http://livingnewdeal.berkeley.edu/resources/timeline/.

14. *National Broadcasting Co., Inc. v. United States*, 319 U.S. 190 (1943).

15. *Yakus v. United States*, 321 U.S. 414 (1944).

16. *United States v. Rock Royal Cooperative, Inc.*, 307 U.S. 533 (1939).

17. Schoenbrod, *Power Without Responsibility*, 4 (quoting John Steinbeck, *The Grapes of Wrath*).

18. Ibid.

19. Ibid., 50.

20. Schoenbrod says five hundred dollars, although that was in 1993. Schoenbrod, *Power Without Responsibility*, 7.

21. Ibid., 4-9, 49-57.

22. Ibid., 52.

23. Robert A. Levy and William H. Mellor, *The Dirty Dozen: How Twelve Supreme Court Cases Radically Expanded Government and Eroded Freedom* (New York: Sentinel, 2008), 81.

24. Ibid.

25. 33 C.F.R. 328.2(b) (Army Corps of Engineers definition); 40 C.F.R. 230.3(t) (EPA definition).

26. *Sackett v. United States Environmental Protection Agency*, 132 S. Ct. 1367 (2012) (Alito, J., concurring).

27. Jerry Taylor, "The Role of Congress in Monitoring Administrative Rulemaking," Cato Institute, September 12, 1996, http://www.cato.org/publications/congressional-testimony/role-congress-monitoring-administrative-rulemaking.
28. *United States v. Mills*, 817 F. Supp. 1546, 1548 (N.D. Fla. 1993).
29. Ibid., at 1546.
30. John C. Coffee, Jr., *"Does 'Unlawful' Mean 'Criminal'?"* Boston University Law Review 71 (1991): 216.
31. Ibid.
32. *Mistretta v. United States*, 488 U.S. 361 (1989).
33. *United States v. Mills*, 817 F. Supp. 1546 (N.D. Fla. 1993).
34. Taylor, "Role of Congress in Monitoring Administrative Rulemaking."
35. Levy and Mellor, *Dirty Dozen*, 68–69.
36. Schoenbrod, *Power Without Responsibility*, 31 (quoting de Tocqueville).
37. Edward H. Crane & David Boaz (eds.), *Cato Handbook for Congress, 108th Congress* (Cato Institute, 2003), 81 (quoting Weisberg).
38. David W. Kreutzer, et al., "What Boxer-Kerry Will Cost the Economy" (Backgrounder #2365 on Cap and Trade), Heritage Foundation, January 26, 2010, http://www.heritage.org/research/reports/2010/01/what-boxer-kerry-will-cost-the-economy; see also "'Cap & Trade': National Energy Tax," U.S. Congressman Bill Posey, http://posey.house.gov/issues/issue/?IssueID=5031.
39. *Immigration and Naturalization Service v. Chadha*, 462 U.S. 919 (1983).

CHAPTER 4: The Supreme Court's Klansman

Sources for the founding-era sections of this chapter include David G. McCullough, *John Adams* (New York: Simon & Schuster, 2001); Akil Reed Amar, *The Bill of Rights: Creation and Reconstruction* (New Haven and London: Yale University Press, 1998); James H. Hutson, *Church and State in America: The First Two Centuries* (Cambridge: Cambridge University Press, 2008); Leo Pfeffer, *Church, State, and Freedom*, Rev. ed. (Boston: Beacon Press, 1967); George C. Homans, "John Adams and the Constitution of Massachusetts," *Proceedings of the American Philosophical Society* 125, no. 4 (August 21, 1981): 286–91; Robert J. Taylor, "Construction of the Massachusetts Constitution,"

Proceedings of the American Antiquarian Society 90, no. 2 (October 1981): 317–46, http://www.americanantiquarian.org/proceedings/44517652 .pdf; *Wallace v. Jaffree*, 472 U.S. 38 (1985) (Rehnquist, J., dissenting); and *Lee v. Weisman*, 505 U.S. 577 (1992) (Scalia, J., dissenting).

The main source for the Hugo Black sections of this chapter is Roger K. New-man, *Hugo Black: A Biography* (New York: Pantheon Books, 1994). Other sources include Noah Feldman, *Scorpions: The Battles and Triumphs of FDR's Great Supreme Court Justices* (New York: Twelve, 2010); Daniel L. Dreisbach, "The Mythical 'Wall of Separation': How a Misused Metaphor Changed Church-State Law, Policy, and Discourse," *Heritage Foundation: First Principle Series*, June 23, 2006; Philip Hamburger, *Separation of Church and State* (Cambridge, Mass.: Harvard University Press, 2002); and *Wallace v. Jaffree*, 472 U.S. 38 (1985) (Rehnquist, J., dissenting) (did not require "that the Government be absolutely neutral as between religion and irreligion").

1. *Wallace v. Jaffree*, 472 U.S. 38 (1985) (Rehnquist, J., dissenting).
2. Hutson, *Church and State in America*, 167.
3. "The First Thanksgiving," Rediscovering George Washington, PBS, http://www.pbs.org/georgewashington/milestones/thanksgiving _about.html.
4. *Wallace*, 472 U.S. 38 (Rehnquist, J., dissenting).
5. *McCreary County v. American Civil Liberties Union of Kentucky*, 545 U.S. 844 (2005).
6. *County of Allegheny v. American Civil Liberties Union*, 492 U.S. 573 (1989).
7. *Robinson v. City of Edmond*, 68 F.3d 1226 (10th Cir. 1995); *Friedman v. Board of County Commissioners of Bernalillo County*, 781 F.2d 777 (10th Cir. 1985) (en banc); *Harris v. City of Zion*, 927 F.2d 1401 (7th Cir. 1991); *Kuhn v. City of Rolling Meadows*, 927 F.2d 1401 (7th Cir. 1991); *Webb v. City of Republic*, 55 F. Supp. 2d 994 (W.D. Mo. 1999).
8. *Engel v. Vitale*, 374 U.S. 421 (1962).
9. *Wallace*, 472 U.S. 38.
10. *Reed v. Van Hoven*, 237 F. Supp. 48, 55 (W.D. Mich. 1965).
11. *Wallace*, 472 U.S. 38 (Rehnquist, J., dissenting).
12. Ibid.
13. Ibid.
14. Ibid.

15. Ibid.
16. Ibid.
17. *Lee v. Weisman*, 505 U.S. 577, 645 (1992) (Scalia, J., dissenting).
18. Ibid.
19. "Columbus Day 2012," Student News Daily, October 8, 2012, http://www.studentnewsdaily.com/daily-news-article/colombus-day-2012/.
20. "Charter to Sir Walter Raleigh: 1584," Avalon Project, http://avalon.law.yale.edu/16th_century/raleigh.asp.
21. "The First Charter of Virginia; April 10, 1606," Avalon Project, http://avalon.law.yale.edu/17th_century/va01.asp.
22. "Mayflower Compact: 1620," Avalon Project, http://avalon.law.yale.edu/17th_century/mayflower.asp.
23. Amar, *Bill of Rights*, 32–33.
24. Hutson, *Church and State in America*, 105.
25. Pfeffer, *Church, State, and Freedom*, 118.
26. Ralph Ketcham (ed.), *Selected Writings of James Madison* (United States: Hackett Publishing, 2006), 164-165.
27. Joseph Story, *Commentaries on the Constitution 3*:§§ 1865–73 (1833), reprinted in Philip B. Kurland & Ralph Lerner, *The Founders' Constitution: Volume Five: Amendments I-XII* (Indianapolis: Liberty Fund, 1987).
28. Dialogue, details, and other historical information for the sections of this chapter about Hugo Black's time in Birmingham come from Newman, *Hugo Black*. This chapter owes a large debt to Newman's excellent book.
29. Newman, *Hugo Black*, 89-90.
30. Ibid., 90.
31. This part of the oath is quoted from Dreisbach, "Mythical 'Wall of Separation,'" 6 n. 10 (quoting Hamburger, *Separation of Church and State*). Other dialogue and details of this section of the chapter come from Newman, *Hugo Black*; and Feldman, *Scorpions*.
32. By the time of Black's nomination, he had sent a resignation letter to the KKK. But as Noah Feldman writes, "Black's resignation letter, designed to be disclosed only in case of crisis, was signed with a Klan salutation that referred to the 'sacred, unfailing bond'—implying that the bond outlasted the purported resignation." Feldman, *Scorpions*, 140.
33. Ibid., 150.

34. Two of them later switched their votes. Newman, *Hugo Black,* 362. Why Black did not then switch with them is unclear. It is impossible to know with certainty why Black took the actions that he took.

35. This part of the oath is quoted from Dreisbach, "Mythical 'Wall of Separation.'"

36. Newman, *Hugo Black,* 362.

37. *Everson v. Board of Education,* 330 U.S. 1 (1947).

38. Francis D. Cogliano, *Thomas Jefferson: Reputation and Legacy* (Edinburgh: Edinburgh University Press, 2006), 6.

39. Hutson, *Church and State in America,* 187.

40. *Wallace,* 472 U.S. 38, 103 (Rehnquist, J., dissenting).

41. Hutson, *Church and State in America,* 183.

42. *Wallace,* 472 U.S. 38, 104 (Rehnquist, J., dissenting).

43. Alexis de Tocqueville, *Democracy in America,* (New York: Penguin Classics, 2003) (Gerald Bevan, transl.), 342.

44. Barbara A. Perry, "Justice Hugo Black and the Wall of Separation Between Church and State," *Journal of Church and State* 31 (1989): 55 (quoted in Philip Hamburger, "Separation and Interpretation," *Journal of Law & Politics* 18 (2002): 7).

45. *Board of Education v. Allen,* 392 U.S. 236, 251 (1968) (Black, J., dissenting).

46. Newman, *Hugo Black,* 100.

CHAPTER 5: Liberty: "A Reality or a Shadow"?

The following sources provided information for the chapter's retelling of John Wilkes's story: Louis Kronenberger, *The Extraordinary Mr. Wilkes: His Life and Times* (Garden City, N.Y.: Doubleday, 1974); Arthur H. Cash, *John Wilkes: The Scandalous Father of Civil Liberty* (New Haven: Yale University Press, 2006); Akil Reed Amar, *The Bill of Rights: Creation and Reconstruction* (New Haven and London: Yale University Press, 1998); Akhil Reed Amar, "Fourth Amendment First Principles," *Harvard Law Review* 107 (1994): 757; Pauline Maier, "John Wilkes and the American Disillusionment with Britain," *William and Mary Quarterly* 20, no. 3 (1963); Jack Lynch, "Wilkes, Liberty, and Number 45," *Colonial Williamsburg Journal,* Summer 2003; Daniel McCarthy, "In Praise of John Wilkes: How a Filthy, Philandering Deadbeat Helped Secure British and American Liberty," *Reason,* July 2006, http://reason.com/archives/2006/07/01/in-praise-of-john-wilkes.

The following sources provided information for the chapter's description of the NSA's domestic spying programs: *Klayman v. Obama*, 957 F. Supp. 2d 1 (2013); Barton Gellman and Laura Poitras, "U.S., British Intelligence Mining Data from Nine U.S. Internet Companies in Broad Secret Program," *Washington Post*, June 7, 2013, http://www.washingtonpost.com/investiga tions/us-intelligence-mining-data-from-nine-us-internet-companies-in -broad-secret-program/2013/06/06/3a0c0da8-cebf-11e2-8845-d970ccb044 97_story.html; Glenn Greenwald, "NSA Collecting Phone Records of Millions of Verizon Customers Daily," *Guardian*, June 6, 2013, http://www .theguardian.com/world/2013/jun/06/nsa-phone-records-verizon-court -order; Barton Gellman, "Edward Snowden, After Months of NSA Revelations, Says His Mission's Accomplished," *Washington Post*, December 23, 2013, http://www.washingtonpost.com/world/national-security/edward-snow den-after-months-of-nsa-revelations-says-his-missions-ac complished/2013/12/23/49fc36de-6c1c-11e3-a523-fe73f0ff6b8d_story.html; Lisa Graves, "Return to Nixonland: How the NSA Slipped Its Leash Under Bush and Obama," *In These Times*, October 17, 2013, http://inthesetimes .com/article/15737/return_to_nixonland_nsa_spying; Aaron Blake and Ellen Nakashima, "Bill Seeks Limits on Call Data Collection," *Washington Post*, June 25, 2013; Ellen Nakashima and Peter Finn, "Lawmakers Who Warned About Phone-Data Collection Seek More Disclosure," *Washington Post*, June 14, 2013; Karen Tumulty, "Reaction to News of Government Actions Blurs Party Lines," *Washington Post*, June 11, 2013; Rand Paul, "Our Liberty Is Being Taken," *Guardian*, June 8, 2013; Robert Pear, "Federal Power to Intercept Messages Is Extended," *New York Times*, December 29, 2012; Ellen Nakashima, "Debate Looms on Electronic-Intercept Law," *Washington Post*, December 9, 2012; "Are They Allowed to Do That? A Breakdown of Selected Government Surveillance Programs," Brennan Center for Justice at New York University School of Law, http://www.brennancenter.org/sites/default/files /analysis/Government%20Surveillance%20Factsheet.pdf; "Reform the Patriot Act: Section 215," American Civil Liberties Union, https://www.aclu .org/free-speech-national-security-technology-and-liberty/reform-patriot -act-section-215; Steve Contorno, "James Clapper's Testimony One Year Later," PolitiFact, March 11, 2014, http://www.politifact.com/truth-o-meter /article/2014/mar/11/james-clappers-testimony-one-year-later/.

1. Kronenberger, *Extraordinary Mr. Wilkes*, 18 ("Her chronic and heraldic injunction was 'George, be King!'").

2. Cash, *John Wilkes*, 79 (quoting *North Briton* 33).

3. Ibid.

4. Lynch, "Wilkes, Liberty, and Number 45" (quoting *North Briton*).

5. Ibid.

6. Cash, *John Wilkes*, 95 (quoting *North Briton* 44).

7. Kronenberger, *Extraordinary Mr. Wilkes*, 135.

8. Cash, *John Wilkes*, 2.

9. Kronenberger, *Extraordinary Mr. Wilkes*, 89.

10. Ibid, 164.

11. Cash, *John Wilkes*, 108.

12. Ibid., 110.

13. Ibid., 115.

14. Ibid., 115–16.

15. Ibid., 119.

16. Ibid., 117–18.

17. Amar, *Bill of Rights, 69.*

18. Cash, *John Wilkes*, 160.

19. Ibid.

20. It appears the jury verdict was for one thousand pounds. Ibid. But Halifax was eventually required to pay four thousand pounds. Amar, "Fourth Amendment First Principles," 781.

21. Amar, "Fourth Amendment First Principles," 814; "Computing 'Real Value' over Time with a Conversion Between U.K. Pounds and U.S. Dollars, 1774 to Present," MeasuringWorth.com, http://www.measuring worth.com/calculators/exchange/result_exchange.php.

22. Cash, *John Wilkes*, 162.

23. Ibid., 116.

24. Ibid., 160.

25. Kronenberger, *Extraordinary Mr. Wilkes*, 135.

26. Ibid., 140.

27. Maier, *John Wilkes and the American Disillusionment with Britain.*

28. Ibid.

29. Amar, "Fourth Amendment First Principles," 772.

30. Ibid.

31. Amar, *Bill of Rights*, 74.

32. *Klayman*, 957 F. Supp. 2d 1, 16.

33. Gellman, "Edward Snowden, After Months of NSA Revelations."

34. USA PATRIOT Act, section 215, codified at 50 U.S. Code 1861.

35. *Klayman*, 957 F. Supp. 2d 1.
36. Ibid.
37. Ibid.
38. Ibid.
39. Ibid.
40. Contorno, "James Clapper's Testimony One Year Later."
41. Ibid.
42. Ibid. Director Clapper's letter to Senator Feinstein on June 21, 2013, can be read at http://abcnews.go.com/Politics/page/letter-sen-feinstein -19560328.
43. Graves, "Return to Nixonland."
44. Ibid.
45. Senate Select Committee to Study Governmental Operations, "Intelligence Activities and the Rights of Americans," Final Report of the Select Committee to Study Governmental Operations with Respect to Intelligence Activities, Book II, 94th Cong., 2d sess., 1976, S. Rep. 94-755, 6.
46. Ibid., 9.
47. *Camara v. Municipal Court*, 387 U.S. 523, 528 (1967).

CHAPTER 6: "But Structure Means Liberty"

1. Robert V. Remini, *Andrew Jackson, vol. 1, The Course of American Empire: 1767–1821* (Baltimore and London: Johns Hopkins University Press, 1998), 141. Remini's excellent biography is the source for much of the material about Jackson in this chapter, including Jackson's duel.
2. William Osborn Stoddard, *Andrew Jackson and Martin Van Buren* (New York: Frederick A. Stokes Company, 2009), 217.
3. Robert V. Remini, *Andrew Jackson, vol. 2, The Course of American Freedom: 1822–1832* (Baltimore and London: Johns Hopkins University Press, 1981), 256.
4. Remini, *Andrew Jackson, vol. 2, Course of American Freedom*, 253.
5. Ibid., 254; "Andrew Jackson, 'Veto of Maysville Road Bill' (1830)," Pinzler, http://pinzler.com/ushistory/vetoofmaysupp.html.
6. Remini, *Andrew Jackson, vol. 2, Course of American Freedom*, 256.
7. Ibid.
8. Remini, *Andrew Jackson, vol. 1, Course of American Empire*, 1–2 (quoting James Parton).

9. Ibid.

10. Jeff Shesol, *Supreme Power: Franklin Roosevelt vs. the Supreme Court* (New York: W.W. Norton, 2010), 2.

11. Shesol, *Supreme Power*, 2.

12. *Schechter Poultry Corp. v. United States*, 295 U.S. 495, 550 (1935).

13. "Fireside Chat on Reorganization of the Judiciary, March 9, 1937," Franklin D. Roosevelt Presidential Museum and Library, http://docs .fdrlibrary.marist.edu/030937.html.

14. *Marbury v. Madison*, 5 U.S. 137 (1803).

15. In a case decided on March 29, 1937, a majority of the Court found a controversial *state* regulation of the minimum wage to be constitutional. *West Coast Hotel v. Parrish*, 300 U.S. 379 (1937). Although this was a flip from a previous pre-Court-packing-plan decision, it was not a flip on the commerce clause, because it concerned a *state* regulation, rather than a *federal* regulation. There was never any doubt that states could regulate intrastate commerce (so long as the regulation did not contravene a part of the U.S. Constitution). Thus, even after *West Coast Hotel*, there was still a meaningful limit on federal power because the Court's commerce-clause jurisprudence still distinguished between intrastate and interstate commerce. That changed on April 12, 1937.

16. *National Labor Relations Board v. Jones & Laughlin Steel Corp.*, 301 U.S. 1, 37 (1937).

17. Transcript of Oral Argument, *Department of Health and Human Services v. Florida*, No. 11-398, United States Supreme Court, March 27, 2012, http://www.supremecourt.gov/oral_arguments/argument_tran scripts/11-398-Tuesday.pdf

CHAPTER 7: Reclaiming the Constitution Through the Courts

The most important sources for this chapter are Brian L. Frye, "The Peculiar Story of *United States v. Miller*," *New York University Journal of Law & Liberty* 3 (2008): 48; Marcia Coyle, *The Roberts Court* (New York: Simon & Schuster, 2013); Brian Doherty, *Gun Control on Trial: Inside the Supreme Court Battle over the Second Amendment* (Washington, D.C.: Cato Institute, 2008); Joyce Lee Malcolm, "The Right of the People to Keep and Bear Arms: The Common Law Tradition," *Hastings Constitutional Law Quarterly* 10 (1983): 285. Much of the substance is taken from the history those sources describe. Dialogue and quotations from the sections about *United States v. Miller* are from Frye.

1. *Marbury v. Madison*, 5 U.S. 137 (1803).
2. Malcolm, "Right of the People."
3. Ibid. ("As his subjects and the republican army of some 60,000 men waited, "armed to the teeth," to greet their new monarch, Charles II found himself virtually unarmed. . . . He was painfully aware that many of these same citizens had gathered for his father's execution eleven years earlier. . . . A study sent to his Court recommended the removal of that power. The anonymous author argued that no prince could be safe 'where Lords and Commons are capable of revolt,' hence it was essential to disarm the populace and establish a professional army. . . . Charles agreed completely.").
4. Ibid. ("There can be little doubt that it was the intention of the promoters of the Game Act to give themselves the power to disarm their tenants and neighbors and to bolster the position of their class with respect to that of the King and of the wealthy members of the middle class.")
5. "An Act for the better preservation of the Game, and for secureing Warrens not inclosed, and the severall Fishings of this Realme," available at http://www.british-history.ac.uk/report.aspx?compid=47447.
6. *District of Columbia v. Heller*, 554 U.S. 570, 594 (2008) (quoting 1 Blackstone 140 (1765)).
7. *Heller*, 554 U.S. at 594.
8. Doherty, *Gun Control on Trial*, 7 (quoting *Federalist 28*).
9. Frye, "Peculiar Story of *United States v.* Miller," 58.
10. Frye, "Peculiar Story of *United States v.* Miller," 52-53.
11. Frye, "Peculiar Story of *United States v. Miller*," 63.
12. Frye, "Peculiar Story of *United States v. Miller*," 64.
13. Frye, "Peculiar Story of *United States v. Miller*," 63-65.
14. Frye, "Peculiar Story of *United States v. Miller*," 67.
15. *United States v. Miller*, 307 U.S. 174 (1939). By my calculations, approximately 69 percent of the opinion consists of quotations, and approximately 5 percent consists of string cites. *See also* Frye, "Peculiar Story of *United States v. Miller*."
16. Doherty, *Gun Control On Trial*, 18.
17. John Paul Stevens, "The Five Extra Words That Can Fix The Second Amendment," *Washington Post*, April 11, 2014, http://www.washing

tonpost.com/opinions/the-five-extra-words-that-can-fix-the-second
-amendment/2014/04/11/f8a19578-b8fa-11e3-96ae-f2c36d2b1245
_story.html

18. Cass R. Sunstein, "The Most Mysterious Right," *New Republic*, November 18, 2007, http://www.newrepublic.com/article/books-and
-arts/archive/76368/second-amendment-gun-rights.

19. Ibid., 24.

20. Coyle, *Roberts Court*, 128 (quoting Neily).

21. Doherty, *Gun Control on Trial*, 85.

22. Coyle, *Roberts Court*, 126 (quoting Ashcroft).

23. Doherty, *Gun Control on Trial*, 65-68.

24. Paul Duggan, "Man at Center of Gun Lawsuit Gets Permit," *Washington Post*, August 18, 2008, http://www.washingtonpost.com/wp
-dyn/content/article/2008/08/18/AR2008081801004.html. See also
the final photograph and caption in Doherty, *Gun Control on Trial*.

CHAPTER 8: Reclaiming the Constitution Through Legislation

1. "*The Economist*/YouGov Poll: Weekly Tracking," August 30–September 1, 2014, 6, http://d25d2506sfb94s.cloudfront.net/cumulus_uploads
/document/b357ahtwtq/trackingreport.pdf.

2. Philip Bump, "Who's as Unpopular as Vladimir Putin? Congress!"
Washington Post, August 6, 2014, http://www.washingtonpost.com
/blogs/the-fix/wp/2014/08/06/vladimir-putin-is-deeply-unpopular-in
-america-like-as-unpopular-as-congress/.

3. Testimony of David Schoenbrod, Hearing before the Subcommittee
on Courts, Commercial and Administrative Law, House of Representatives, March 8, 2011, http://www.gpo.gov/fdsys/pkg/CHRG-112
hhrg65074/html/CHRG-112hhrg65074.htm.

4. Additional reforms would also be necessary. For example, the REINS
Act would operate only prospectively and would itself do nothing to
rein in regulations in effect prior to its passage. But once this reform is
in place, preexisting regulations could be run through the REINS Act
filter by a separate reform providing for their sunset after a specified
period of time.

CHAPTER 9: Reclaiming the Constitution Through the Power of the Purse

1. John R. Graham, "Obamacare's Employer Mandate Delay Creates Two Big Problems," *Forbes*, July 27, 2013, http://www.forbes.com/sites /theapothecary/2013/07/27/obamacares-employer-m/.

2. Julian Zelizer, "How Congress Got Us Out of Vietnam," *American Prospect*, February 19, 2007, http://prospect.org/article/how-congress -got-us-out-vietnam.

3. "Can Appropriations Bills Defund Obamacare?" *Heritage Foundation*, August 14, 2013, http://www.heritage.org/research/factsheets/2013/08/ can-appropriations-bills-defund-obamacare.

4. Todd Garvey, "Closing Yucca Mountain: Litigation Associated with Attempts to Abandon the Planned Nuclear Waste Repository," *Congressional Research Service*, June 4, 2012, http://www.fas.org/sgp/crs /misc/R41675.pdf.

5. *Patient Protection and Affordable Care Act*, HR 3590, 111th Cong., 2nd sess., section 1332. Available at http://www.gpo.gov/fdsys/pkg/BILLS -111hr3590enr/pdf/BILLS-111hr3590enr.pdf.

6. *Department of Defense and Full Year Continuing Appropriations Act, 2011*, Public Law 112-10, 112th Cong., section 1857. Available at http://www.gpo.gov/fdsys/pkg/PLAW-112publ10/html/PLAW -112publ10.htm.

7. Kelly Phillips Erb, "Government Shutdown 101: What Happens When the Lights Go Off?" *Forbes*, September 20, 2013, http://www .forbes.com/sites/kellyphillipserb/2013/09/20/government-shutdown -101-what-happens-when-the-lights-go-off/.

8. Perianne Boring, "Regulating the Citizenry: What Really Happened During the Partial Government Shutdown," *Forbes*, October 17, 2013, http://www.forbes.com/sites/perianneboring/2013/10/17/regulating -the-citizenry-what-really-happened-during-the-partial-government -shutdown/ (reporting that 18 percent of the federal workforce was furloughed); Holly Yan, "Government Shutdown: Get Up to Speed in 20 Questions," CNN, October 1, 2013, http://www.cnn.com/2013/09 /30/politics/government-shutdown-up-to-speed/ (reporting that 800,000 of 3.3 million government workers are furloughed during a shutdown).

9. Erb, "Government Shutdown 101."

10. Boring, "Regulating the Citizenry."

11. John Tozzi, "Obamacare's Year of Delayed Deadlines," *Bloomberg Businessweek*, March 13, 2014, http://www.businessweek.com/printer /articles/189307-obamacares-year-of-delayed-deadlines; Sarah Hurtubise, "The Definitive Roundup of Obamacare's Worst Delays," *Daily Caller*, March 31, 2014, http://dailycaller.com/2014/03/31/the-definitive -roundup-of-obamacares-worst-delays/.

CHAPTER 10: What *You* Can Do to Reclaim the Constitution

1. Gordon Lloyd, "Stage V: A Long Hot Summer: Nail Biting Time," *Ratification of the Constitution: The Six Stages of Ratification*, Teaching AmericanHistory.org, http://teachingamericanhistory.org/ratification /stagefive/.
2. "The Debates in the Convention of the State of New York, on the Adoption of the Federal Constitution," Constitution Society, http:// www.constitution.org/rc/rat_ny.htm.
3. Ronald Reagan, "The New Republican Party," 4th Annual CPAC Convention, Washington, D.C., February 6, 1977, available at http:// reagan2020.us/speeches/The_New_Republican_Party.asp.
4. Hon. Donetta W. Ambrose, "Reflections on a Career," *The Side Bar*, December 2010, 2, available at http://www.westbar.org/pdf/xxii06 .pdf.
5. Matthew 10:16.
6. Genesis 2:17; Genesis 3:5.
7. Matthew 10:16.
8. Whittaker Chambers, *Witness* (Washington, D.C.: Regnery Publishing, 1952), 25, 541.
9. Letter from George Washington to Bushrod Washington, November 10, 1787, available at http://oll.libertyfund.org/titles/2415.

INDEX

Abdülhamid I, Sultan, 48
abortion, 2–5
Adams, John, 22, 77, 100, 101
  Massachusetts Constitution and,
    81–85
Adams, Samuel, 86
agrarian society criticism of
    Constitution, 10
Agricultural Marketing Agree-
    ment Act, 64
air pollution, 8, 67–68
Ali, Muhammad, 126
Alito, Samuel Anthony, 151, 153,
    209
American Civil Liberties Union, 74
Anti-Federalists, 86–87, 119, 132
Aristotle, 159
arms, right to bear. *See* Second
    Amendment
Army Corps of Engineers, 69
Articles of Confederation, 19–21
Ashcroft, John, 169

Bedford, Gunning, 31
Bill of Rights, England, 160, 161
Bill of Rights, U.S., 85–88,
    118–19
  First Amendment, 77–102

Fourteenth Amendment's
    applicability to, 94–95
Fourth Amendment, 103–29
ratification of, 162
Second Amendment, 158–74
Tenth Amendment, 87, 95,
    131–53
Bipartisan Campaign Reform Act
    of 2002 (McCain-Feingold
    Act), 11–12
Black, Hugo Lafayette, 89–102
  appointed to Supreme Court, 94
  Everson decision, 96–101
  as Ku Klux Klan member,
    93–94, 101–2
  McCollum decision, 100
  Stephenson case and, 89–92
Blackstone, William, 160
Blaine Amendment, 95–96
Block, Lawrence, 71–72
Boston Massacre, 116, 117
Boston Tea Party, 116
Bradley, Bill, 74
Briton, 105
budgeting and appropriations
    process, 191–93
Burger, Warren, 166–68, 169
Burr, Aaron, 60
Bush, George W., 11–12

Bute, Lord, 106
Butler, Pierce, 38

Camden, Lord. *See* Pratt, John,
    Lord Chief Justice
cap-and-trade, 74
Carlos IV, King, 47
Catherine the Great, 47–48
Catholic Church/Catholicism,
    88–92, 95–99, 101
Causici, Enrico, 210, 211, 212
Chambers, Whittaker, 215
Charles II, King, 159, 161
Christmas créche/nativity scenes,
    78, 80
Church Committee, 126
Churchill, Winston, 215
Cicero, 159
*City of Akron v. Akron Center for
    Reproductive Health*, 3
Civil Aeronautics Board, 64
Clapper, James, 120–21, 124–25
Clay, Henry, 136–37, 138, 139,
    141, 142
Clean Air Act, 8, 67–68, 74
Clean Water Act, 68–70
Code of Federal Regulations,
    179–80
Columbus, Christopher, 83
Commerce Clause, 133, 144–45,
    149–52
Committee for Purchase from
    People Who Are Blind or
    Severely Disabled, 73
Congress
    under Articles of Confederation,
        19–20
budgeting and appropriations
    process, 191–93
contacting, on constitutional
    issues, 203–6
delegation of legislative powers
    to executive agencies, under
    Roosevelt, 61–67
domestic spying, proposals to
    rein in, 180–81
electing representatives/senators
    that will uphold Constitu-
    tion, 206–9
failure to uphold and defend
    Constitution, 9–11
government shutdown, 193–96
impeachment powers of, 208–9
legislative power of, 47–75
limited powers of (*See* Tenth
    Amendment)
Obama's usurpation of legislative
    powers of, 188–90, 196–97
privacy rights of Americans,
    protection of, 180–85
proposed Regulations from the
    Executive in Need of
    Scrutiny Act (REINS)
    requiring rulemaking by,
    177–80
role of, in reclaiming Constitu-
    tion, 175–97
rule- and regulation-making
    powers delegated to federal
    agencies by, 7–9
state representation in, 17–19,
    22–32
unpopularity of, 175
Constitution, U.S. *See also* Bill of
    Rights

agrarian society criticism of, 10
citizenry's' role in reclaiming,
199–216
Commerce Clause, 133–34,
144–45, 149–52
Establishment Clause, 77–102
failure of Congress to uphold
and defend, 9–11
federalism and, 204–5
Hamilton's arguments in favor of
ratification of, 199–200
judiciary's role in reclaiming,
157–74
legislative branch's role in
reclaiming, 175–85
Legislative Powers Clause,
47–75
oath to preserve, protect and
defend, 9
Origination Clause, 17–45
reading of, encouraging, 203
Washington on, 215–16
Constitutional Convention
Hamilton's executive for life
proposal, 53–58
Legislative Powers Clause,
origins and background of,
47–61
Madison's call for, 19–21
New Jersey Plan, 25–26, 59–60
Origination Clause solution to
representation issue, 33–39
quorum call, 21–24
resolution calling for, 20
scope of delegates authority at,
24–25
state representation in Congress
debate, 17–19, 22–32

Virginia Plan, 24, 59–60
Washington as chairman, 24
Contras, 189
Cooper, Myles, 50–52
court-packing plan, of Roosevelt,
146–47
Coyle, James, 88–89
Cromwell, Oliver, 159
crony capitalism, 66

data collection program, NSA,
121–25, 127, 128
Dean, Gordon, 164
Declaration of Independence, 22,
23, 50
Defund Obamacare campaign,
190–97
Democrats
government shutdown and,
193–96
REINS Act and, 177–78
Department of Agriculture, 65, 66
Depression, 61–62
Dickinson, Charles, 134–36, 139
Dickinson, John, 39
Diderot, Denis, 19
District of Columbia
firearms laws of, challenge to,
168–74
representation in Congress issue,
10
District of Columbia v. Heller,
171–74
domestic spying
Congress's role in reining in,
180–85
by NSA, 121–25, 127, 128

Durbin, Dick, 184
Dust Bowl, 65

Egremont, Lord, 105
elections, 206–9, 213–214
Electronic Communications
    Privacy Act of 1986, 181
Ellsworth, Oliver, 30–31
e-mail, 181
Encyclopedia (Diderot), 19
Environmental Protection Agency
    (EPA), 8–9, 67–68, 69, 74
Equal Employment Opportunity
    Commission, 73
Establishment Clause, 77–102
    Black's interpretation of, in
        *Everson v. Board of Educa-
        tion*, 96–101
    drafting and purpose of, 85–88
    historical interpretation of,
        77–78
    judicial misinterpretation of,
        78–79
    role of religion in founding era
        and, 81–85
    state right to establish religion,
        79–80
Everson v. Board of Education,
    96–101
executive agencies, 7–9, 61–73
    Congress' delegation of legisla-
        tive powers to, under
        Roosevelt, 61–67
    judicial failure to combat
        lawmaking by, 70–71
    proposed Regulations from the
        Executive in Need of

Scrutiny Act (REINS)
    requiring Congressional
    rulemaking, 177–80
    regulatory compliance costs
        imposed by, 71–73
executive branch
    legislative powers of Congress
        ceded to, 61–67
    oath of office, 9

Farm Credit Administration, 64
Farm Security Administration, 64
Federal Communications Com-
    mission, 64
Federal Deposit Insurance
    Corporation, 64
Federal Housing Administration, 64
federalism, 204–5
Federalist Papers, 43, 49, 128, 162,
    179, 187, 207, 213
Federalists, 132
Federal National Mortgage
    Association, 64
Federal Savings and Loan Insur-
    ance Corporation, 64
firearms, right to bear. *See* Second
    Amendment
First Amendment, 77–102
    Establishment Clause (*See*
        Establishment Clause)
    Free Exercise Clause, 97
FISA Amendments Act, 184
Food and Drug Administration
    (FDA), 71
Foreign Affairs, 175
Foreign Intelligence Surveillance
    Court (FISA), 122, 181

forty-five, 117–18
Fourteenth Amendment, 94–95
Fourth Amendment, 103–29
  drafting of, 118–20
  modern abuses of power in U.S.,
    examples of, 125–28
  NSA data collection program
    and, 121–25, 127, 128
  Wilkes' struggle for liberty in
    Britain as inspiration for,
    106–18
Frankfurter, Felix, 63
Franklin, Benjamin, 18, 23,
  28–29, 31, 32–37, 47, 57, 115

Game Act (England), 159, 160
generally, 118–20
general warrants, 104, 108–9,
  113–14, 118–19, 128
George III, King, 25, 48, 50, 103,
  104–5, 106, 161
Gerry, Elbridge, 35, 37, 38, 39
Glorious Revolution, 160, 161
government shutdown, 193–96
Grapes of Wrath, The (Steinbeck), 65
Gulf of Tonkin Resolution, 189
Gussman, Pedro, 89, 91–92
Gutensohn, Paul, 164–65

Halifax, Lord, 107–9, 113, 114
Hamilton, Alexander, 21, 29, 75
  argues for ratification of Consti-
    tution, 199–200
  Cooper lynch mob and, 50–52
  on executive power, 53–58
  on right of self-defense, 162

health care reform, 40–45
Heller, Dick, 170–74, 200
Henry, Patrick, 59, 86
Home Alone (movie), 2
Hoover, Herbert, 148
House Resolution 3590 (Service
  Members Home Ownership
  Tax Act of 2009), 42–43,
  44–45
Hughes, Charles Evan, 148

Ienari, Tokugawa, Shogun, 48
impeachment, 208–9
individual mandate, Obamacare,
  150–53
Intolerable Acts, 116–17
IRS denial of tax-exempt status to
  conservative nonprofit
  organizations, 127

Jackson, Andrew, 133, 134–42
  duel with Dickinson, 134–36
  limited federal government,
    belief in, 136–42
  Maysville Road Bill veto and,
    138–41
James II, King, 160, 161
Jefferson, Thomas, 19, 22, 78,
  99–100
judiciary, 157–74. See also Supreme
  Court
  authority and role of; Marbury v.
    Madison, 157, 158
  Second Amendment and,
    158–74
Judiciary Act, 157

Kaskaskia Indians, 78

Kennedy, Anthony, 150–51, 153, 172–73, 203

King, Martin Luther, Jr., 126

Ku Klux Klan, 88, 89–94

Landis, James, 63–64, 178

Lansing, John, 57

Layton, Frank, 162–64

Leahy, Pat, 180, 181

legislative branch. *See* Congress

Legislative Powers Clause, 47–75

  Congress' transfer of legislative power to Roosevelt's agencies, 61–67

  designing a republic and, 47–49

  executive agency rulemaking and, 7–9, 61–73

  Hamilton's executive for life proposal, 53–58

  Madison's Virginia Plan and, 59–60

Leon, Richard, 124

Levy, Robert, 168–71, 172–73, 174, 200

Liberty and the Eagle (sculpture), 210–12, 214

Locke, John, 63, 81

Louis XVI, King, 47

lynch mob, and Hamilton, 50–52

McCain-Feingold Act (Bipartisan Campaign Reform Act of 2002), 11–12

McCollum v. Board of Education, 100

McDougall, Alexander, 117–18

McReynolds, James Clark, 164–66

Madison, James, 50, 56, 57, 77, 100

  Articles of Confederation, reform of and, 19–21, 22, 23, 28, 29, 30

  Bill of Rights and, 85–88, 118, 119

  on dangers of voluminous laws, 179–80

  on House of Representatives power of the purse, 43, 187

  legislative powers issue and, 58–60

  on need for checks and balances, 213

  on scope of federal government's powers, 207

  on separation of powers, 49

Marbury v. Madison, 146–47, 157, 158

Maria, Queen, 47

Marshall, John, 146–47, 157, 158

Martin, Luther, 26–28, 29–30, 34, 35

Martin, Samuel, 105–6

Mary II of England, 160, 161

Mason, George, 31–32, 35, 37, 38

Massachusetts Constitution, 81–85

  Declaration of Rights, 82–84

  religion, establishment of and, 82–84

  separation of powers in, 82

Mayflower Compact, 83–84

Maysville Road Bill, 138–41

Miller, Jack, 162–64
Mills, Carey, 69–70, 71
Mills, Ocie, 69–70, 71
Mitchell, Andrea, 125
Montesquieu, Charles de, 63, 81

National Firearms Act, 162–66
National Industrial Recovery Act,
  143–44
National Journal, 124
National Labor Relations Board,
  64
National Labor Relations Board v.
  Jones & Laughlin Steel,
  147–48
National Recovery Administra-
  tion, 144
National Rifle Association
  (NRA), 167, 169
National Security Agency (NSA),
  120–25, 127, 128
National Security Letters, 180–81
Naval Orange Administrative
  Committee, 66
Neily, Clark, 168–70, 172–73,
  200
New Deal, 63–64, 143–49, 163,
  178
New Jersey Plan, 25–26, 59–60
New Republic, 74
New York, 199–200
New York Times, The, 126
Nicaragua, 189
Nixon, Richard, 167
North Briton, 105–6, 107–8, 112,
  114, 116
nuclear waste storage, 189–90

oaths of office, 9
Obama, Barack, 40–42, 45, 74,
  127, 188–90, 193, 194, 195,
  196–97
Obamacare. See Patient Protection
  and Affordable Care Act
Occupational Safety and Health
  Administration, 73
Office of English Language
  Acquisition, 73
Office of Price Administration,
  64
Ogden, Nicholas, 50
orange quotas, 65–66
Origination Clause, 17–45
  attempts to remove and final
    compromise for, 37–39
  Franklin's introduction of, 33–37
  health care reform and, 40–45
  state representation debate and,
    17–19, 22–32
Overton, Thomas, 134, 135

parochial schools, 78, 80, 95–99,
  101
Paterson, William, 24–26, 34, 35
Patient Protection and Affordable
  Care Act, 42–45, 150–53,
  187–97
  defunding campaign and,
    190–97
  employer mandate of, 188–89
  government shutdown and,
    193–96
  individual mandate of, 150–53
  Obama's rewriting of, 188–90,
    196–97

PATRIOT ACT, 120, 122, 180–84
Paul, Rand, 184
Pinckney, Charles, 37
Pitt, William, 103
police power, 131–32
Pratt, John, Lord Chief Justice, 110–11, 112, 113, 118
prayer, 77, 78, 80
privacy rights of Americans, protection of, 180–85
probable cause, 119
Putin, Vladimir, 175

Qianlong Emperor, 48

Ragon, Hiram, 163–64
Raleigh, Walter, 83
Randolph, Edmund, 21, 24, 38, 39
Rangel, Charlie, 42
Reagan, Ronald, 189, 201
Regulations from the Executive in Need of Scrutiny Act (REINS) (proposed), 177–80, 200–201
regulatory compliance costs, 71–73
Reid, Harry, 43–44, 45, 189–90, 191
religion
Establishment Clause and (See Establishment Clause)
Free Exercise Clause, 97
role of, in founding era, 81–85
Republicans
failure to defend Constitution of, 11

government shutdown and, 195–96
REINS Act and, 177–78
Roberts, John, 152
Roberts, Owen, 148–49
Roger, Vinson, 70–71
Roosevelt, Franklin Delano, 73, 94
Congress's ceding of legislative powers to, 61–67
federal government power, scope of, 133–34
Supreme Court and, 142–49

St. Georges Fields Massacre, 114, 117
Scalia, Antonin, 80, 153, 173–74
Schoenbrod, David, 65
Second Amendment, 158–74
Burger on, 166–68, 169
District of Columbia firearms laws, challenge to, 168–74
National Firearms Act, constitutionality of, 162–66
origins of, in English Bill of Rights, 159–62
Second Continental Congress, 22
Securities and Exchange Commission, 64
separation of powers, 49, 74–75
in Massachusetts Constitution, 82
Service Members Home Ownership Tax Act of 2009 (House Resolution 3590), 42–43, 44–45
Sherman, Roger, 30
Simpson, Steve, 168–70, 172–73

Social Security Administration, 64
Stamp Act, 116
states
  religion, establishment of (*See*
    Establishment Clause)
  representation of, in Congress,
    17–19, 22–32
Steinbeck, John, 65
Stephenson, Edwin, 88–92, 101
Stewart, Jimmy, 215
Stewart, Potter, 79, 101
Stone, Harlan Fiske, 94
Story, Joseph, 87, 100
Sunkist, 66
Supreme Court, 9
  Congressional delegation of
    legislative powers and,
    70–71
  court-packing plan of Roosevelt
    and, 146–47
  Establishment Clause and,
    96–101
  on Fourth Amendment's
    purpose, 128
  on individual right to bear arms;
    District of Columbia v. Heller,
    171–74
  McCain-Feingold provisions
    invalidated by, 12
  on National Firearms Act;
    United States v. Miller,
    164–66
  oath of office, 9
  Roosevelt and, 142–49

Taft, William Howard, 148
taxation
  Articles of Confederation and,
    20
  Obamacare upheld under
    Congress's power of, 152–53
  Origination Clause and state
    representation in, 22–39
  regulatory compliance costs as
    hidden, 71–73
Ten Commandments, 78
Tenth Amendment, 87, 95, 131–53
  background and drafting of,
    131–33
  Commerce Clause argument for
    expanding federal powers
    and, 133, 144–45, 149–52
  Jackson and, 133, 136–42
  Obamacare and, 150–53
  Roosevelt and, 133–34
Thomas, Clarence, 101, 153
Tocqueville, Alexis de, 73, 100
trespass suit, of Wilkes against
  Lord Halifax, 112–14, 118
Tribe, Laurence, 167
Troup, Robert, 50, 52

United States v. Miller, 164–66
U.S. Housing Authority, 64
USA Freedom Act (proposed),
  180, 200–201
USA PATRIOT ACT, 120, 122,
  180–84

Van Buren, Martin, 137, 139
Verizon, 122
Verrilli, Donald B., Jr., 151
Vietnam War, 189

Virginia Declaration of Rights, 81

Virginia Plan, 24, 59–60

wall of separation between Church
    and State, 99–101

Walpole, Horace, 116

warrants

    Fourth Amendment require-
        ments, 118–20

    general, 104, 108–9, 113–14,
        118–19, 128

    probable cause requirement, 119

Washington, George, 18, 21, 24,
    53–54, 77, 100, 136, 215–16

Washington Post, 126

Weisberg, Jacob, 74

*Why John Roberts Was Wrong About
    Healthcare: A Conservative
    Critique of the Supreme
    Court's Obamacare Ruling*
    (Lee), 153

Wilhelm III, Frederick, King, 47

Wilkes, John, 103, 104, 106–16,
    128, 129

    arrest of, under general warrant,
        108–9

    colonists inspired by, 116–18

    continued prosecutions of, and
        growing public support for,
        114–16

    North Briton Number 45,
        publication of, 107–8, 114

    raid of home of, 111–12

    trespass suit against Lord
        Halifax of, 112–14, 118

William of Orange, 160, 161

writs of assistance, 116

Wyden, Ron, 120, 121, 124

Yates, Robert, 57

Yucca Mountain, 189–90